GREEN GUID

Birds

OF BRITAIN AND EUROPE

To Jim - in memory of our
lovely holiday in Porlock.
June 1992. Sitting on the
beach - milking the sun;
climbing through Selworthy
woods to the marvellous views
of sea and moor; foxgloves -
coastal flowers - the huge
breakfasts of "Lavender Cottage
sleeping to the sound of the sea
Sheba content in a "Watership
Down" landscape; wine and
roses................... ∴

GREEN GUIDE

Birds

OF BRITAIN AND EUROPE

JIM FLEGG
ILLUSTRATED BY MARTIN WOODCOCK

AURA BOOKS

This edition first published in the UK in 1992 by
New Holland (Publishers) Ltd
37 Connaught Street, London W2 2AZ
in association with Aura Books plc

ISBN 1 85368 167 9 (hbk)
ISBN 1 85368 161 X (pbk)

Commissioning editor: Charlotte Parry-Crooke
Editor: Ann Baggaley
Designer: Paul Wood

Phototypeset by AKM Associates (UK) Ltd
Reproduction by Scantrans Pte Ltd
Printed and bound in Singapore by
Kyodo Printing Co (Singapore) Pte Ltd

Contents

Introduction

The beauty of birdwatching is its simplicity – whether you are walking along the pavement or standing in a garden or park there will always be birds to watch. Birds are highly mobile, so there is always the chance of catching the unexpected – the brilliant streak of a Kingfisher darting along the riverbank or the muffled wingbeats of a group of swans flying low overhead. All you need is a keen eye, some basic equipment, and a guidebook such as this designed to help you identify the bird and understand something about its lifestyle and habitat.

The more that can be gleaned about how and where birds live, the more fascinating and rewarding this hobby will become. This guide will help you both to identify a bird correctly and to understand why and how such a bird was found at a particular time and place. It covers 150 of the species most likely to be seen in Britain and Europe, each with an individual illustration, easy-to-follow field notes to confirm identification and a map showing its main distribution.

The maps show the distribution for each species, using the following colour codes:
Blue   Winter visitors
Yellow   Summer visitors' breeding range
Green   All year-round presence

The symbols which appear on the illustrations indicate the sexes and plumage variations:

♂ Male
♀ Female
I Immature
S Summer plumage
W Winter plumage

How to Identify Birds

The shape of a bird is geared for flight and the basic body-plan of a bird differs little from species to species. The majority of birds are small, and the larger they are the more energy-saving their flight becomes.

The skeleton of a bird is made up of a strong central 'box' of backbone, ribs and breastbone. The vital organs are grouped within for protection and to form a centre of gravity between the wings that helps make flight much easier.

The wings, which are attached to this central box, are the most distinctive and identifiable feature of birds. The outline varies tremendously and is an invaluable aid to identification, especially when the outline of the bird may only be seen in flight. Game birds have rounded wings for quick take-off and short escape flights; birds of prey, on the other hand, have broad wings with heavily fingered tips to catch air thermals so they can glide effortlessly when searching for prey or during long migrations. Seabirds that habitually skim the rolling waves of the oceans, such as the Fulmar, have long, straight and narrow wings.

Feathers are unique to birds and are remarkable structures made of a protein called keratin. They are not just indispensable to successful flight, but also make the bird wind- and water-proof and provide thermal insulation. The colours and markings of feathers give birds excellent camouflage or dazzling display plumages for courtship – all of which adds another valuable clue to the identification of a particular species, and perhaps reveals its age or sex.

Tails vary as much as wings and are also a valuable marker for instant identification. They are essentially for steering, but are also

Introduction

used in courtship displays; and the way they are held, their colour and shape offer useful guides.

At the other end of the bird, the beak varies according to what the bird uses it for – the long decurved bill of the Curlew is for probing, while that of the Great Spotted Woodpecker is for chiselling, and that of the Goldfinch acts as a pair of tweezers. Beaks can be especially helpful in differentiating similar-looking species such as ducks, where one species may be a fish-eating 'sawbill' and another a broad-billed filter feeder.

Legs and feet are the last but by no means least valuable appendages to aid successful bird identification. As with beaks, the range of shapes reflects different lifestyles. Herons have long legs, ideally suited to wading, while the razor-sharp talons of raptors and owls are superbly designed to grab and kill prey; the webbed toes of divers and ducks are designed for efficient swimming.

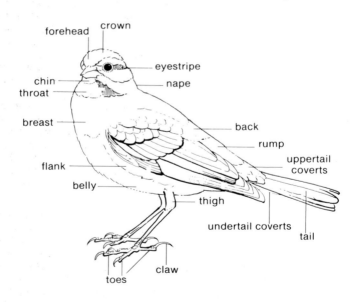

Bird Habitats

The power of flight has enabled birds to spread themselves over almost all the earth's surfaces. Insects may be more widely dispersed on land, but not many are found at sea. Birds, on the other hand, are found from the tropical oceans to the icy polar waters, above mountain-tops and in deep valleys.

Although birds can flit between habitats and turn up almost anywhere – particularly during the migration season or just after stormy weather when they may have been blown off course – it is essential to recognise the basic bird habitats just to anticipate what sort of bird you may wish to see, as well as to make identification easier.

Contrary to popular belief, if a particular species chooses to inhabitat a man-made landscape, this does not make it an uninteresting bird to watch. A number of quite surprising bird species have managed to penetrate human abodes such as villages, towns and even cities, and have adapted to them quite successfully. The hazards of traffic and domestic animals are outweighed by the abundance of cultivated food and scraps as well as the milder climate that urban conglomerations generate. Starlings and House Sparrows may predominate in such areas, but the odd Jackdaw, Greenfinch or Great Tit may also be spotted. If you have a garden and can put out a bird table, then a wider variety of species will be attracted – Robins, Song Thrushes and Blue Tits perhaps. The garden is a great magnet for birds, but municipal parks are good habitats for Woodpigeons and Tawny Owls, while city lakes will attract waterbirds such as Moorhens, Coot, Canada Geese, Mute Swans and several species of duck. Feral pigeons are ubiquitous and perhaps not welcome, but their relative, the Collared Dove, is a newcomer that has made an impressive move to farmland and cultivated surroundings from the Middle East over the past 50 years.

Further afield, farmland provides many species of birds with a diverse rural habitat, despite the trend towards prairie-type farming and the widespread use of pesticides and fertilisers. The combination of field, hedgerow and woodland edge that many farms provide, suits a great number of species including thrushes, finches and buntings, as well as seed-eating birds like the Linnet and the Yellowhammer and migrant warblers like the Whitethroat. Not many species favour the wide-open monoculture crop fields, with the notable exception of the Skylark. Farm buildings provide welcome nest sites for Spotted Flycatchers, Swallows, Wagtails and, if the buildings are old, the rapidly declining Barn Owl.

Introduction

As for the woodlands themselves, broadleaved trees such as oak, ash and beech attract owls as well as the Sparrowhawk. Neither is easy to find. The seasonal abundance of insects in the canopy will attract many year-round residents such as tits, but also migrants including the Turtle Dove and many warblers.

The more widely-spaced coniferous woodlands are good places to spot Coal Tits, Redstarts and Woodpeckers. The paucity of undergrowth does not deter the likes of Goldcrests and Chaffinches as well as Woodpigeons. Freshly planted or cleared forests attract the Tree Pipit and other unexpected birds.

Freshwater habitats or wetlands – from humble hill streams to mighty river estuaries as well as ponds, lakes, marshes and reservoirs – offer a wonderful variety of birdlife for the bird-watcher. On upland streams you may enjoy the sight of Common Sandpipers, Dippers and Grey Wagtails forever bobbing their tails or bodies on mid-stream boulders or pebbly banks scanning for food. The Kingfisher, too, may flash past. Waders such as the Redshank and Snipe will be seen in marshes and lowland rivers. Natural wetlands provide among the richest variety of bird species, but man-made reservoirs also make excellent, if not scenic, bird-watching sites with huge varieties of wintering waterfowl and the odd exotic migrant. Where the river finally joins the sea, the combination of brackish, sheltered, relatively warm water rich in nutrients is a magnet for wildfowl, gulls and waders in autumn, winter and spring. Many of these species are overwintering here before making their long-haul flights. Estuaries are essentially staging posts for such birds, so it makes sense to plan a field trip according to the seasonal migrations. Such an abundance of similar-looking species in close proximity can present a considerable problem when attempts are made to identify them.

From spectacular cliff faces and rock stacks facing the brunt of the Atlantic storms to the more sheltered low-lying mudflats, the coastline of Europe is very exposed and so attracts specific groups of birds such as auks and gulls. In the summer months the bird-watcher's rewards can be magnificent, especially where there are colonies of breeding seabirds like Gannets. Cliff-top walks or boat trip forays will afford spectacular aerial views and ample opportunity to watch differing plunge-dive techniques of fishing birds. This is also an excellent chance to study differing courtship and nesting techniques be it Puffins in cavities or Guillemots on flat ledges. In winter, waders and wildfowl predominate.

Scrub, heathland and moors are good spots to watch various warblers, pipits, shrikes and the Hoopoe. Bushes and brambles provide abundant nest sites for song and perching birds. Meadow Pipits are much in evidence in moorland as are the Golden Plover and Dunlin. With few trees, birds must nest on the ground and rely on camouflage against would-be predators such as foxes or stoats. Year-round moorland residents include Red Grouse.

The mountain areas of Europe are effectively ecological islands combining a mixture of Mediterranean and Arctic habitats suited to Buzzards and Golden Eagles swirling on upcurrents. The latter's home territory may cover some hundred square kilometres, as it ranges in search of prey to satisfy its food demands. Catching sight of such a bird is one of the true joys of birdwatching.

Practical Birdwatching and Conservation

Stealth – the ability to come up close to a bird without disturbing it – is probably the most useful attribute a would-be birdwatcher can hope to master. Birds have exceptionally keen eyesight and hearing (though fortunately their chances of picking up human scent in the wind are remote) and will disappear into a frustrating blur just as the watcher settles down for a good look. So the first rule of good fieldcraft is always to move quietly. In woodland, obviously, it is important to avoid crashing through undergrowth, snapping twigs underfoot.

Listening is almost as crucial as moving slowly. If you pause frequently to listen you will hear the various bird songs and calls that will give advance warning of what species to expect. Of course, much of this knowledge comes with experience, but tapes of bird calls, can be bought, or borrowed from a library, and the notes in this book contain the most common calls. Most birds are heard before they are seen, so learning to recognise the key repertoire of calls is a great asset.

Remember to walk slowly and take advantage of the natural cover provided by trees, bushes and other vegetation. When you reach a gap, pause to listen for a few moments, then look around. The birds will reveal themselves. It may sound obvious, but even experienced birdwatchers can forget where they are and suddenly pull out a handkerchief, scaring off any nearby birds.

Just as birds are well camouflaged in their natural habitats, so too the aspiring birdwatcher should wear dull browns or greens and certainly not ultrabright anoraks or loud rustling plastic kagouls. It is hard enough not drawing attention to yourself as you creep through the undergrowth so there is no point in advertising your presence by unsuitable outdoor clothing.

The *Concise Guide* will help you to plan a field trip, as it explains which species are likely to be seen in the type of habitat you have chosen to visit. A field note book is also indispensable for jotting down the essential characteristics of your sighting: size, colourings, markings, wing shape, tail shape, beak shape, plus any distinctive markings such as eyestripes or wingbars. Make a note of the bird call, using a phonetic spelling; also make a note of the habitat, time of day, month, and the species and numbers of each bird seen.

Birdwatching can be enjoyed without specialist equipment such as a telescope, tripod, single-lens reflex camera with telephoto lens and cassette recorder – but a pair of binoculars is an essential which will

literally open up a whole new avian world. A specialist camera/binocular shop will advise on technical details such as the most suitable magnification.

The most important consideration when birdwatching is to put the birds' interests first: never disturb nesting birds or tired migrants. Kites and divers, for example, are suffering directly because of birdwatchers' activities during their breeding season. The need to get near to a bird does not mean that wild vegetation should be trampled underfoot or other wildlife scared off in the process. Wildlife habitats are precariously balanced these days and you should always be aware of not upsetting the delicate ecological balance in the pursuit of birdwatching. Any rubbish should be taken home for disposal – a casually discarded plastic wrapping can be a lethal time-bomb for an unsuspecting bird. It also goes without saying that you should be aware that birds and eggs are protected by law, and that effective prosecutions, leading to substantial fines, are now the routine.

You can help birds in a positive way by joining and giving financial support to one of the many bird clubs, societies and trusts that have become strong lobbying pressure groups. Bird societies also spend a large part of that financial support in setting up and maintaining a network of bird reserves that goes a long way to conserving both disappearing habitats and endangered species. Joining a local ornithological group will help conservation at grass-roots level. You can offer to collect data on local bird numbers and movements which is of great practical assistance to both the scientific study of birds and their conservation, locally *and* nationally.

Bird Classification and Characteristics

There is an accepted scientific naming system for birds (as for all animals and plants) which has the great advantage of being understood internationally, even if the bird's common name differs from country to country. For example, a British birdwatcher may call that popular songbird of our gardens with the red breast a 'Robin', but this would not mean much to a French bird spotter who knows it as *'Rouge-gorge'*. The scientific name *Erithacus rubecula*, however, is known worldwide, not just in Europe. To an American, on the other hand, the name 'Robin' means a different species altogether as clearly identified by its scientific name *Turdus migratorius*. But the classification system does more than this: it helps us identify bird species by placing them in a series of groupings. First there is the species; then closely-related species are grouped in the same genus. A genus that is related to another genus is then placed in a family grouping, and families in turn are combined into the largest grouping called orders.

The key to understanding these groups is to remember that they are partly based on structural similarities that generally speaking would be obvious to the birdwatcher in the field. So, for example, the large forward-looking eyes, disc-like face, hooked bill and sharp taloned feet of the owls place them in the order Strigiformes, and the families Tytonidae and Strigidae. Recognising such family likeness will certainly aid birdwatchers in the field. The species described in this book belong to the following groups.

Divers (order Gaviiformes, family Gaviidae)
As their name suggests, diving birds of the water with streamlined bodies, long necks, and dagger-shaped beaks. In flight their silhouette resembles a cigar and their rapidly beating wings are a good identification pointer.

Grebes (order Podicipediformes, family Podicipedidae)
Smaller and plumper diving waterbirds with rather shorter dagger-like beaks. They have stumpy, fluffy tails. Most of their body is submerged when swimming.

Tubenoses (order Procellariiformes)
Oceanic seabirds that get their name from the prominent paired tubular nostrils on the ridge of the beak that also looks segmented. Shearwaters and Fulmars glide low over the water on stiff wings, while Storm Petrels flutter low over the waves, dipping down to pick food off the surface.

Gannet and Cormorants (order Pelecaniformes)
Enormous waterbirds with huge feet. The spectacular black and white Gannet has slim pointed wings and plunge-dives into the sea from great heights. The dark and slim-bodied Cormorants are often seen standing on rocks with wings outstretched to dry.

Herons (order Ciconiiformes)
Wading birds with long legs, slender toes and long necks found along marshes and coasts. They stab at prey with their dagger beaks. Their wings are broad and heavily fingered and they fly with slow steady wingbeats at quite fast speeds.

Introduction

Waterfowl – swans, geese and ducks – (order Anseriformes)
All have webbed feet and three forward-pointing toes. The generally
duck-like beaks are the other identifying feature. Swans are the
largest in this order with their recognisable long necks and adult
white plumage. Geese are somewhat smaller and are identifiable by
their flying in 'V' formation and honking calls. Ducks have short
necks with feet set well back on the body which gives their tell-tale
waddling walk. The wings are fast beating and pointed at the tip.
Ducks differ from other waterfowl in that the male and female have
different plumages (the male is usually the more distinctive). The
exception to this, and the short neck, is the Shelduck.

Birds of Prey (orders Accipitriformes and Falconiformes)
Often called raptors, they have powerful hooked beaks for tearing
flesh, large eyes for locating prey and long legs with strong talons
and sharp claws at the end for killing prey. All raptors have a fleshy
pad called a cere, at the base of the beak, which contains the nostrils.
As it takes several years to reach maturity, with irregular moults,
there is a confusing variation of juvenile plumages. Females are
generally larger than males.

Game Birds (order Galliformes)
Heavy set with small heads and chicken-like beaks. Their wings are
round and fingered which gives them almost vertical take-off as
well as their distinctive whirring flight.

Rails (order Gruiformes)
Dumpy wetland birds with long spidery toes that are often lifted
well out of the water in their sedate walk. Most have a short, stout
beak.

Waders, Shorebirds (part of order Charadriiformes)
The birds belonging to the order Charadriiformes are classified together because of anatomical features that are not obvious to the birdwatcher. Waders have long legs and horizontally-held bodies. Length and colour of legs and bills, and plumage details, especially wingbar, rump and tail patterns help to distinguish the species, as do their diverse feeding techniques.

Skuas (part of order Charadriiformes)
Gull-like seabirds characterised by the white flashes in the centre of the wings noticeable in flight. They have a faster dashing flight than gulls, and harry other seabirds for food.

Gulls (part of order Charadriiformes)
They have long legs with webbed feet and comparatively long wings. Male and female adults are usually white bodied with back and wings grey or black. Fine details of shape, size and plumage will assist identification of individual species.

Terns (part of order Charadriiformes)
Smaller than gulls with shorter necks, slimmer wings and shorter legs. Their name 'sea swallows' comes from their graceful flight. They often hover above the water before diving to plunge just beneath the surface for prey. Marsh terns, such as Black Terns, also hawk for insects over wetlands.

Auks (part of order Charadriiformes)
Stout strong-billed birds with webbed feet set far back on the body and small wings that whirr in low flight above the sea. They are superficially penguin-like when they stand erect.

Pigeons and Doves (order Columbiformes, family Columbidae)
Relatively heavy-bodied birds with small heads and beaks on longish necks. Their tails are long and wings pointed.

Owls (order Strigiformes, families Tytonidae and Strigidae)
They have large round heads, a distinctive facial disc with hooked beak and round eyes, and a characteristically neckless appearance. Body plumage tends to conceal their long legs but their feathered toes have strong sharp talons. Their eerie calls and generally nocturnal habits also single them out for identification.

Introduction

Cuckoos (order Cuculiformes, family Cuclidae)
Elusive medium-sized, long-tailed birds with short pointed wings giving them a flight silhouette like a falcon, but they can be distinguished by their small, weak, unhooked bills and their calls.

Kingfishers and Hoopoe (order Coraciiformes)
Brightly coloured birds whose individual plumage makes identification easy. Common features are scarce, except that they are hole-nesters.

Woodpeckers (order Piciformes, family Picidae)
Possess stout dagger-shaped beaks and climb trees in a head-uppermost position with long claws on their two-forward, two-back toes providing excellent grip. Plumage is generally a striking black, white and red, sometimes green ·and yellow. All are hole-nesters.

Swallows and Martins (order Passeriformes, family Hirundinidae)
All have relatively long curved wings with a recognisable forked tail. They will perch readily, which the similar Swift does not.

Swifts (order Apodiformes, family Apodidae)
Wings are distinctively long and sickle-shaped. Swifts live almost entirely on the wing. The dark body is shaped like a torpedo with a short tail and tiny legs.

Larks (order Passeriformes, family Alaudidae)
Well camouflaged, ground-nesting, mottled brown birds with long hind claws. They have a song-flight which aids identification. Beak shapes vary according to diet.

Pipits and Wagtails (order Passeriformes, family Motacillidae)
Spend much of their time running after insects. Wagtails are small
and slim-bodied with a long white-bordered tail that they wag up
and down continuously. They are boldly patterned while Pipits by
contrast are generally brownish and well streaked but inconspicuous. Pipits have a distinctive song-flight. Song and habitat help to
distinguish the species.

Accentors (order Passeriformes, family Prunellidae)
Small, shy inconspicuous birds with drab plumage. Knowing their
habitat and song can aid correct identification.

Dipper (order Passeriformes, family Cinclidae)
Only one species, which has a large white bib and a habit of bobbing
on boulders before plunging into rivers.

Wren (order Passeriformes, family Troglodytidae)
Only one species, with a tiny cocked tail, chestnut colours and a
short-range whirring flight. The song is powerful and melodious.

Thrushes and Chats (order Passeriformes, family Turdidae)
Plump, strong-legged birds with medium-thick beaks for eating
fruit, insects, snails and worms. Distinctive plumage helps distinguish the various members, which include Robins, redstarts, chats,
wheatears and thrushes.

Introduction

Warblers and Crests (order Passeriformes, family Sylviidae)
All have finely pointed, often slim beaks for eating insects. Most are
summer visitors. While some are melodious warblers, as their name
implies, others produce a scratchy, metallic sound – so knowledge of
song will help to differentiate the species.

Flycatchers (order Passeriformes, family Muscicapidae)
Summer visitors. They have slim beaks when viewed side-on, but
broad-based when viewed from above or below. They have
prominent bristles surrounding their gape. Their slim body has
long wings and very short legs. They catch insects in flight,
returning to a prominent perch. Plumage helps identification.

Tits (order Passeriformes, families Timaliidae, Aegithalidae,
Paridae)
Three families, two of which are very distinctive. The true tits have
stubby, sharply-pointed beaks and are tree dwellers. Their weak
flight with bursts of fluttering wingbeats is a good field guide, as are
their individual plumage markings and song. The Bearded Tit and
Long-tailed Tit have plumages which are difficult to mistake.

Treecreepers (order Passeriformes, family Certhiidae)
Move woodpecker-like on tree trunks, head-up with stiff tail acting as a prop. The beak is downcurved and finely pointed and the large eyes are set below a marked eyebrow. In flight the prominent wingbar pattern provides a good field guide.

Nuthatches (order Passeriformes, family Sittidae)
Resemble woodpeckers and have stout dagger-like beaks. They move with equal ease in a head-down or head-up pose. Toes are three forward, one back. The tail is soft and does not serve as a prop.

Shrikes (order Passeriformes, family Laniidae)
Have bold plumage with striking wingbars, long tails and hawk-like hooked beaks. Another characteristic is the habit of impaling prey temporarily on thorns or barbed wire.

Crows (order Passeriformes, family Corvidae)
Black or black and grey birds, usually with a metallic sheen. Their beaks are stout. They are prone to hopping about the ground when scavenging. Jays and Magpies are more strikingly plumaged members of this group.

Starlings (order Passeriformes, family Sturnidae)
Among the most ubiquitous of birds in urban and country habitats. Their glossy iridescent greens and purples, and direct flight on triangular wings, are useful guides to identification.

Finches (order Passeriformes, family Fringillidae)
Noticeable for their short triangular or wedge-shaped beaks, well adapted to crushing varying types of seed. Undulating flight and a forked tail in some species can also aid recognition.

Buntings (order Passeriformes, family Emberizidae)
Superficially resemble elongated and colourful Sparrows with thickish wedge-shaped beaks. The lower jaw is larger than the upper. Distinctive summer plumages and song help distinguish the males. The duller females and immatures are difficult to identify.

Sparrows (order Passeriformes, family Passeridae)
Small, stocky birds with robust wedge-shaped beaks for seed eating. Most have a drab plumage and undulating flight.

Red-throated Diver *Gavia stellata* 55cm Smallest diver. Summer adult has grey-brown back, sparse, pale markings; underparts white. Head grey-brown. Neck white, dark brown streaks. Throat-patch dark red, appearing almost black. Beak pale; dagger-shaped, slightly upturned, held upwards. Winter adult greyish above, white flecking; white below. Immature resembles winter adult. In flight, slimmer and paler than other species, wingbeats more rapid and deeper. Cackling and barking calls during breeding season, silent in winter. Breeds beside moorland pools, occasionally by sea inlets. Occurs inshore along west European coast. Widespread, rarely numerous.

Little Grebe *Tachybaptus ruficollis* 25cm Smallest and dumpiest of the grebes. Short-necked and characteristically tail-less appearance. Summer adult dark brown, with chin and upper throat rich chestnut, and small yellow patch at base of beak. Winter adult drab brown above, paler below. Immature resembles winter adult. Far-carrying, shrill whinnying song. Found year-round on slow-moving rivers, canals, ditches, lakes and man-made waters, usually with ample marginal vegetation. Common and widespread.

Great Crested Grebe *Podiceps cristatus* 45cm Largest of the grebes. Summer adult grey-brown above, white below. Head conspicuously crested and tufted in chestnut and black. Neck white, long and slender. Beak orange, dagger-like. Winter adult generally greyer, with only slight indication of crest. Immature resembles winter adult. In flight appears hump-backed, and shows conspicuous white patches on whirring wings. Various guttural honks and croaks accompany display. Frequents larger reed-fringed fresh waters year-round; some winter on sheltered coastal waters. Widespread, fairly common.

Fulmar *Fulmarus glacialis* 45cm Heavy-bodied seabird, well streamlined. Adult and immature superficially gull-like in plumage, pale grey above shading to white below. Wings lack black tips. Beak yellowish, with tubular nostrils on ridge. Flies on short, straight wings, often held downcurved. Glides extensively, with few wingbeats except close to the cliffs. Various cackling and crooning calls on breeding ledges, silent elsewhere. Breeds colonially on coastal cliff ledges, on ground along remote coastlines, sometimes on buildings. Some remain in coastal waters all year, others disperse to mid-ocean in winter. Widespread, locally numerous.

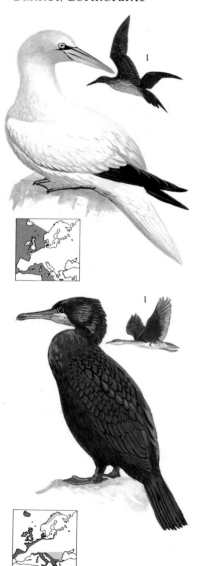

Gannet *Sula bassana* 90cm Huge seabird; long-necked, long-tailed, cigar-shaped body. Adult largely white above and below. Wings black tipped; long, straight, slender and sharply pointed. Head and neck tinged yellow. Beak steel-grey, long, dagger-shaped. Immature grey-brown flecked with white, gradually showing more white as adult plumage is acquired. In flight, characterised by slow, stiff wingbeats, with frequent glides. Plunges spectacularly when hunting fish. Raucous honks and grating calls on breeding grounds, silent elsewhere. Breeds in colonies on remote islands or headlands. Winters in coastal and offshore waters. Widespread, locally numerous.

Cormorant *Phalacrocorax carbo* 90cm Large, long-necked, broad-winged seabird. Adult blackish with metallic sheen. Face (and sometimes thighs) patched with white in summer. Southern European breeding birds may also have white head and neck. Facial skin yellow. Beak yellow and hooked. Winter adult lacks white patches. Immature dark brown above, paler on throat and underparts. Swims low in water, diving frequently. Deep guttural grunts when on breeding grounds. Breeds colonially on islands and cliffs beside shallow seas or estuaries, or in trees beside large inland fresh waters. Overwinters in same habitats. Widespread.

Shag *Phalacrocorax aristotelis* 75cm Large dark seabird, similar to Cormorant but smaller. Summer adult blackish with green iridescent sheen. Shags never show white patches. Curled crest in early spring, traces of which persist into summer. Beak yellow, slim and hooked at tip. Immature brown above and below, appreciably darker-bellied than young Cormorant. In flight, slighter build, slimmer neck and smaller head help separation from Cormorant. Harsh croaks on breeding grounds. Year-round resident on rocky coasts and nearby clear seas. Semi-colonial or solitary breeding bird. Locally common.

Little Egret *Egretta garzetta* 55cm Slender, medium-sized heron. Adult white, with long white crest and fine plumes on back in breeding season. Neck long and slender, usually held extended. Beak black, long and dagger-shaped. Legs black and long with striking and characteristic golden feet. Immature whitish, lacking plumes and crest. Flies with head withdrawn between shoulders but legs extended. Various harsh honks and shrieks, usually confined to breeding season. Inhabits marshland of all types with open water, rivers, saline lagoons. Breeds colonially in mixed 'egretries' in trees. Locally quite common.

25

Grey Heron *Ardea cinerea* 90cm
Huge waterside bird. Adult
blue-grey above; wings grey,
blackish primaries; white
below. Head white, black line
through eye. Neck white,
slender; throat dark-streaked.
Beak yellow, heavy, dagger-
shaped. Breeding adult has
black and white crest, silver-
grey plumes on back, pinkish
flush to beak. Legs yellowish,
long. Immature resembles
adult, lacks crest and plumes.
Flight stately on broad,
heavily-fingered wings, head
retracted, legs extended.
Harsh honks and shrieks,
especially 'fraank', mostly
during breeding season.
Frequents wetlands: ponds,
estuaries, sheltered sea coasts.
Breeds colonially in reedbeds
or trees. Widespread.

Mute Swan *Cygnus olor* 150cm
Huge and unmistakable. Adult
all-white year-round. Neck
long, carried in graceful 'S'
curve. Beak dark orange, with
black knob on forehead larger
in male than female. Adult
raises wings like sails high
over back in defence of
territory or young. Immature
pale grey-buff; beak pinkish-
grey. In flight, long, broad,
heavily-fingered wings creak
loudly. Rarely vocal, hisses or
grunts when annoyed.
Frequents all types of fresh
water larger than ponds,
including town park lakes.
Occasionally found on
sheltered seas. Widespread.

Bewick's Swan *Cygnus columbianus* 120cm Appreciably smaller than other swans. Adult all-white year round. Neck short, straight and goose-like. Beak short, wedge-shaped, largely black with irregularly shaped lemon-yellow patches at base, the pattern, varying between individuals. Immature pale grey, basal patches on beak greyish- or pinkish-yellow. In flight, more buoyant and with faster wingbeats than its larger relatives. Wingbeats silent. Musical goose-like honks and chatterings. Breeds on swampy tundra. Winters on sheltered seas, large freshwater areas and grazing marshes. Scarce, locally numerous on regular wintering grounds.

White-fronted Goose *Anser albifrons* 70cm Medium-sized grey goose. Adult grey-brown above and below, with white beneath the tail; heavy black barring across breast. Head and neck darker brown, with large white face-patch at base of beak. Beak pink (eastern or Russian race) or orange-yellow (western or Greenland race). Legs orange. Immature similar, but lacks white face and breast barring. Noisy, with a gabbling yapping call. Breeds on tundra. Winters on rough grassland, fresh and salt marshes, fields. Widespread, locally numerous.

Geese

Brent Goose *Branta bernicla*
60cm Small, dark, short-necked goose. Adult back blackish-brown, rump black. Tail white with black terminal band. Head and neck sooty black, with small white collar. Breast and belly grey (pale-bellied race *hrota*) or dark grey (dark-bellied race *bernicla*). Undertail white. Beak blackish, small. Legs blackish. Immature similar; pale barring across back, lacks white collar. Gregarious. In flight, white tail conspicuous. Wingbeats quick. Usually flies in irregular, loose flocks. Voice a soft low 'rruuk'. Breeds on Arctic tundra. In winter favours estuaries, sheltered bays and nearby marshes and fields. Widespread, locally numerous.

Canada Goose *Branta canadensis*
75cm Largest of the 'black' geese, almost swan-sized. Adult body dark brown above, paler below, with white patch below black tail. Head and long neck black; white face-patch on cheeks and under chin. Beak black. Legs dark grey. Immature similar to adult, duller. In flight, black rump and white-tail band conspicuous. Wingbeats powerful. Call a hoarse disyllabic 'aah-honk'. Vagrant North American birds winter with grey geese on coastal marshes. Most European birds are descendants of introduced stock; resident on large fresh waters, including park lakes, and nearby grassland. Widespread.

Shelduck *Tadorna tadorna* 60cm
Large, goose-like duck with
striking pied plumage. Adult
predominantly white. Back
has two long black stripes,
belly narrower central black
stripe. Head bottle-green;
neck has broad chestnut band
round base. Beak scarlet, knob
at base larger in male than
female; female may have
whitish patch at base. Legs
pink. Immature has grey
instead of green or black
markings, lacks chestnut
collar. Barking call 'ak-ak-ak'
and deep nasal 'ark'. Seen
year-round on estuaries and
sheltered sandy or muddy
coasts, occasionally on fresh
waters. May breed far from
water. Widespread, often
numerous.

Wigeon *Anas penelope* 45cm
Medium-sized surface-feeding
duck. Adult male has grey
back, finely marked grey
flanks and black undertail.
Breast pink; head chestnut
with gold crown stripe. Beak
grey with black tip; stubby. In
flight shows conspicuous
white oval patch in wing.
Female and immature similar,
a mixture of cinnamon-
browns flecked with darker
markings, showing a greyish
wing-patch in flight. Male
produces a characteristic,
plaintive whistle, female a
low-pitched purr. Breeds on
moorland and tundra close to
water. Winters on lakes,
estuaries and sheltered seas,
and on nearby marshes and
grassland. Widespread and
often common.

Mallard *Anas platyrhynchos* 58cm
One of the larger surface-feeding ducks; best-known duck in Europe. Adult male grey-brown above and below, with black above and below white tail. Rump has curled black feathers. Head bottle-green, separated from chestnut breast by narrow white neck-ring. Beak yellowish-green. Legs orange.

Female and immature speckled brown, buff and black; beak brownish-orange. In flight, all show broad purple speculum-patch between white bars on inner section of wing. Male gives quiet whistle, female harsh quacks. Frequents most waters year-round, from small ponds to open seas. Common, almost ubiquitous.

Teal *Anas crecca* 35cm One of the smallest surface-feeding ducks. Adult male predominantly greyish, flanks have conspicuous white stripe; undertail golden. Breast buff with fine grey barring. Head chestnut, with dark green patch around eye; may appear blackish at a distance. Female and immature similar,

speckled grey-brown. Flight fast and erratic. Male has distinctive low 'krit' call, and strange bell-like whistle; female harsh 'quack'. Breeds on boggy or marshy land with reed-fringed pools. Winters in similar habitats, often well inland, and on estuaries and sheltered coastal waters. Common, often numerous.

Pintail *Anas acuta* 70cm Large surface-feeding duck, slim build, longish neck. Adult male has grey-brown back, white belly, finely marked grey flanks. Tail black, long and pointed. Head and neck rich brown, distinctive white mark on side of neck. Beak and legs grey. Female and immature pale grey-brown marked with darker brown; short, pointed tail. In flight, slender, elongated silhouette; wings narrow, inconspicuous brown speculum on trailing edge. Rarely vocal; male has low whistle, female low quack and churring growl. Breeds on moors and freshwater marshes close to water. Winters on sheltered coastal waters; sometimes inland.

Shoveler *Anas clypeata* 50cm Medium-sized surface-feeding duck. Adult male brown above, white below; chestnut patches on flanks. Short neck and heavily-built head bottle-green. Beak dark grey; massive and spoon-shaped. Female and immature speckled brown, similarly massive beak brownish-orange. All swim low in water, head tilted down. In flight, rapid wingbeats and head-up, tail-down attitude are characteristic; pale grey forewing patches conspicuous. Male has low-pitched double quack 'tuk-tuk', female quiet quack. Breeds on marshland with reed-fringed pools or lakes, winters in similar areas, on reservoirs and sheltered coastal waters. Common.

Ducks

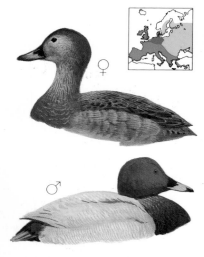

Pochard *Aythya ferina* 45cm
Medium-sized diving duck. Adult male has grey back, and is mostly white below; breast and undertail black. Head dark chestnut. Beak black with grey band near the tip. Female and immature dull rufous-brown, paler on cheeks, throat and belly. Both sexes have steeply rising forehead; wings greyish with an indistinct, paler grey wingbar. Dives frequently. Rarely vocal; male has hoarse whistle, female harsh growl. Breeds beside large reed-fringed fresh waters; winters on large fresh waters including reservoirs, occasionally along sheltered coasts. Common and widespread.

Tufted Duck *Aythya fuligula* 43cm Small, diving duck. Adult male black above; breast black, flanks and belly white; undertail black. Head purplish, crested during breeding season. Female and immature dark brown above, female sometimes with rudimentary crest in breeding season. Older females may have white patch at base of beak. Underparts paler; belly grey-buff. Eyes golden-yellow, beak black-tipped lead-grey in both sexes. In flight, wingbeats rapid; white wingbar conspicuous. Male has soft whistle during breeding season, female low-pitched growl. Breeds beside ponds, ditches, lakes; winters on similar waters; occasionally on sheltered coasts. Common.

Goldeneye *Bucephala clangula*
48cm Medium-sized sea duck.
Adult male predominantly
black above, white below.
Back black; closed wing has
row of white patches often
merging into bar. Head
greenish-black, crested and
angular; small circular white
patch below eye. Female and
immature brown above, flanks
paler, belly whitish. Head
chestnut, angular. Swims
buoyantly, in groups, diving
frequently. In flight, wing
feathers make rattling
whistle; white wing-patches
conspicuous. Rarely vocal;
male occasionally produces
disyllabic nasal call, female
harsh growl. Breeds near
water. Winters coastally or on
inland fresh waters. Regular,
rarely numerous.

Red-breasted Merganser
Mergus serrator 55cm Medium-
sized sawbill duck. Adult male
black above, flanks finely
marked grey, belly white.
Breast chestnut, dark brown
speckling. Head and bristling
crest bottle-green, throat
white, nape black. Beak
orange-red; long, narrow with
serrated edge. Female and
immature grey above, paler
below, belly white. Breast and
throat white, head and nape
chestnut-brown with spiky
crest. Swims low in water,
dives frequently. In flight
black and white wing-patches
conspicuous. Usually silent.
Breeds beside rivers and along
sheltered coasts. Winters
along coasts, also on large
fresh waters. Widespread,
regular, rarely numerous.

Raptors

Black Kite *Milvus migrans* 53cm
Large predominantly dark
kite. Adult and immature
various shades of dark brown;
immature generally paler on
breast. Tail long. Upright
perching posture. In flight,
wings appear long and
relatively narrow, with
fingered tips, usually showing
pale mid-wing patch on
underside; tail often fanned,
showing very shallow fork, or
twisted characteristically.
Flight extremely agile. Social,
often soaring or gathering at
carrion in flocks. Call a
Herring-gull-like mewing.
Frequents forests, but also
urban areas and especially
refuse tips. Widespread, more
numerous in warmer areas.

Marsh Harrier *Circus
aeruginosus* 53cm Large broad-
winged harrier. Adult male
largely brown above,
underparts chestnut. Wings
strikingly patterned, patches
of brown and grey contrasting
with black flight feathers. Tail
pale grey, long. Adult female
largely rich dark brown, with
much creamy-yellow on head.
Immature predominantly
brown with darker streaks,
lacking yellow patches.
Characteristic flight low and
steady, with frequent
extended glides on wings held
stiffly in shallow 'V'. Voice
rarely heard, disyllabic high-
pitched 'kee-ya'.
Characteristically inhabits
marshland with extensive
reed beds. Widespread, locally
common.

Hen Harrier *Circus cyaneus*
48cm Medium-sized harrier.
Adult male pale grey on head,
back and tail, with white
rump-patch. Wings grey with
blackish flight feathers.
Female and immature rich
brown above and below, with
darker streaks; tail long and
brown with narrow dark bars;
large white rump-patch.
Sometimes collects in
communal winter roosts. In
flight and hunting technique
looks similar to Marsh
Harrier, but wings narrower.
Voice, not often heard, a
chattering 'kee-kee-kee'.
Frequents open country, from
moorland and forestry
plantations to farmland and
coastal or inland marshes,
especially in winter.
Widespread, rarely numerous.

Osprey *Pandion haliaetus* 58cm
Medium-sized fish-hunting
raptor. Adult and immature
upperparts brown; wings dark
above, generally pale below
with dark wingtips and 'wrist'
patch. Underparts largely
white; breast has band of
brown streaks. Head white
with large brown patch
through eye. Crown loosely
crested. Beak grey, relatively
small; hooked. Legs and large
feet with powerful long talons
grey. In flight, wings are
characteristically held in an
'M' and arched. Plunge dives
for fish. Voice rarely heard, a
brief whistle. Frequents lakes
and streams, saline lagoons
and man-made fresh waters.
Widespread but rarely
numerous.

35

Buzzard *Buteo buteo* 53cm
Medium-large broad-winged
raptor. Adult and immature
variable in plumage, normally
darkish brown above, whitish
below with heavy darker
streaking. Individuals may be
pale buff above or dark brown
below. Often perches in
upright posture on poles or
trees. In flight, usually dark
'wrist' patch contrasts with
generally pale underwing.
Soaring habits and flight
silhouette are characteristic,
with long, broad, heavily-
fingered wings and short,
dark, fanned tail. Voice a far-
carrying, cat-like mewing.
Inhabits open country,
including farmland and
moorland, with tracts of
woodland. Widespread, locally
common.

Kestrel *Falco tinnunculus* 35cm
Medium-sized falcon. Adult
male has chestnut-brown back
with heavy dark brown spots;
tail grey with black terminal
bar. Underparts buff, with
darker spots. Head grey.
Female and immature brown
above, buffish below, with
heavy brown spots and
streaks. Long pointed wings
may sometimes appear
rounded. Hovers frequently
and expertly. Call a shrill,
repetitive 'kee-kee-kee'.
Habitat widely varied, from
towns and cities, farmland,
marshes, to moors, mountains
and sea coasts. Common.

Golden Eagle *Aquila chrysaetos*
83cm Huge typical and
majestic eagle. Adult
uniformly rich dark brown;
head and nape tinged golden.
Tail comparatively long and
broad. Beak massive and
hooked. Immature wings have
white patches; tail white with
broad, black terminal band.
White areas get smaller with
age, causing possible
confusion with other eagles.
In flight, wings impressively
long, broad and heavily
fingered, held slightly above
horizontal when soaring, but
with tips often curled
downwards. Voice rarely
heard, a barking 'kaah'.
Inhabits remote mountain and
forest areas, down to sea level
in places. Widespread, never
numerous.

Sparrowhawk *Accipiter nisus*
35cm Small dashing hawk.
Male dark grey above; tail
grey with darker bars, long.
Underparts distinctive: throat
white, breast and belly white
but closely barred with
chestnut, appear reddish at a
distance. Crown grey,
sometimes small white nape-
patch. No eyestripe. Female
much larger, grey-brown
above; underparts white,
barred with brown. Eyestripe
white, separating dark crown
and cheeks. Immature
plumage similar to female but
breast has brown streaks, not
barring. In flight, short,
rounded wings and long tail
confer good manoeuvrability.
Call a rapid 'kek-kek-kek'.
Inhabits forests and woodland.
Widespread, often common.

Game Birds

Red-legged Partridge *Alectoris rufa* 35cm Medium-sized game bird. Adult grey-brown above; buffish below, flanks boldly barred with black, white and chestnut. Head strikingly patterned with white chin and upper throat, surrounded by black border and black streaking extending onto breast. Beak and legs bright red. Immature sandy-brown, lacking distinctive head pattern. Flight low and direct on whirring wings. Voice 'chuck, chuck-arr.' Inhabits dry farmland, heath and scrub. Locally common.

Pheasant *Phasianus colchicus* 85cm Large long-tailed game bird. Adult male unmistakable: body iridescent bronze, beautifully marked; tail buff with dark brown bars, very long. Head glossy bottle-green with scarlet face-patches. Female and immature sandy-buff with darker streaks; tail shorter. Flight rapid, with long glides after bursts of flapping; take-off explosive. Male has a ringing 'cork-cork' call followed by loud wing-claps. Inhabits farmland, heath, scrub and open woodland. Widespread, numbers influenced by release of captive-reared birds.

Grey Partridge *Perdix perdix*
30cm Medium-sized game bird.
Adult has buff-streaked
brownish back; face and upper
throat rich chestnut; nape and
breast dove-grey, paling
towards the belly. Flanks have
bold chestnut barring. Dark
brown, inverted horseshoe
patch on belly larger in male
than female. Immature
streaked sandy-brown. Flight
low, direct and fast on
whirring wings, showing
chestnut sides to tail. Voice
'chirrick-chirrick'. Inhabits
arable fields, grassland, heaths
and scrub. Widespread, locally
common.

Red Grouse *Lagopus lagopus*
40cm Medium-sized, skulking
game bird. Adult male (in
Britain) mottled rich reddish-
chestnut above and below;
female drabber. Wings dark
brown in both sexes. Red
fleshy wattles over eyes. Beak
short and stubby. The
continental Willow Grouse
has white wings in summer, is
white with a black tail in
winter. Remains concealed
until threatened; takes off in
whirring flight, short,
downcurved wings beating
fast. Voice a loud 'go-back-
urr'. Inhabits heather
moorland, willow scrub and
tundra edges. Widespread,
locally common.

Crakes

Coot *Fulica atra* 38cm Medium-large crake. Adult uniformly dull velvety black. Forehead has fleshy patch, diagnostically white. Beak short. Legs and feet grey, with distinctive lobed webbing to toes. Immature dark grey-brown above, paler below. Swims buoyantly, diving frequently. Flies low over the water, revealing conspicuous white trailing edges to wings. Voice a single or repeated strident 'kowk'. Inhabits larger expanses of fresh or brackish water, including reservoirs in winter. Occasional on sheltered estuaries. Common.

Water Rail *Rallus aquaticus* 28cm Medium-sized, skulking crake. Adult has upperparts of rich buffish-brown, speckled and streaked with dark brown; predominantly leaden grey on face and underparts, with flanks boldly barred black and white and striking white undertail coverts. Beak reddish, long, slender and slightly downcurved. Legs and toes yellowish, long. Immature darker, more speckled above and barred below. Flies rarely, fluttering low with legs trailing. Various noisy, pig-like grunts and squeals. Inhabits dense reedbeds and heavily vegetated swamps. Widespread, rarely numerous. Difficult to see.

Moorhen *Gallinula chloropus* 33cm Medium-sized crake. Adult velvety brownish-black; flanks have characteristic white streak. Undertail coverts white, conspicuous when tail is jerked while swimming. Forehead scarlet, fleshy. Beak red with yellow tip. Legs and long toes green.

Immature drab grey-brown, darker above than below. Swims well, upends but does not dive. Flies feebly and low over water, legs trailing. Several ringing calls, including 'whittuck'. Inhabits fresh waters from the smallest pool to the largest lake. Common.

Common Snipe *Gallinago gallinago* 28cm Small, long-beaked wader. Adult and immature rich brown, barred and streaked chestnut, buff and black; crown has three bold, yellowish-buff, longitudinal stripes. Beak brownish, straight, very long. Legs greenish, comparatively short. Flight a swift zig-zag when flushed; wingbars and

striped back conspicuous; tail rounded, showing dark band. Display flight soaring and diving, fanned tail produces throbbing, bleating noise. Call on taking flight, a harsh 'scarp'; in breeding season, a clock-like 'tick-er, tick-er'. Breeds on wetlands and moorland. Winters in similar habitats, salt marshes and saline lagoons.

Waders

Black-winged Stilt *Himantopus himantopus* 38cm Medium-sized wader with extremely long legs. Adult has back and wings black, with head, neck and underparts white; nape shows varying amounts of grey or black. Beak black, long and very slender. Legs rich pink, almost ridiculously long, enabling it to wade and feed in deeper water than other waders. Immature browner above; legs greyish-pink. Flight feeble for a wader, showing dark undersides to wings but no wingbars, legs trailing conspicuously well beyond tail. Noisily vociferous with yelping 'kyip' call. Inhabits salt pans, coastal lagoons and marshes. Locally common.

Avocet *Recurvirostra avosetta* 43cm Medium-sized wader, with unmistakable pied plumage and upturned beak. Adult predominantly white above and below, crown and nape black; back and wings have black bars; wingtips black. Beak black; long and extremely slender towards tip, which is markedly upturned. Feeds by sweeping beak from side to side in shallow water. Legs grey, relatively long. Immature similarly patterned but browner. Vocal, with a 'kloo-oot' call varying from flute-like to strident if alarmed. Inhabits saline or brackish lagoons and pools. May overwinter on sheltered estuaries. Locally common. Breeds colonially, often winters in flocks.

Oystercatcher *Haematopus ostralegus* 43cm Conspicuously pied, medium-sized wader. Adult black backed; tail white, with black terminal band; underparts white. Head and neck black. Beak orange, long, fairly stout. Legs and feet pink, thick and fleshy. Winter adult and immature blackish on beak; white collar-mark on neck. In flight, usually in noisy flocks, black wings show conspicuous white wing-bars. Vociferous: various 'kleep' calls and pipings. Breeds on coastal marshes, grassy islands, sand dunes, and on inland damp grassland. Winters on coasts and estuaries. Widespread, often common, usually in flocks in winter.

Lapwing *Vanellus vanellus* 30cm Medium-large plover. Adult black above with purplish-green iridescent sheen; tail white with terminal black bar. Flanks and belly white, undertail coverts rich chestnut. Crown black with conspicuous long, slender, upturned crest. Cheeks greyish, throat and breast black. Beak black and stubby. Legs brown, long. Immature browner, with buff fringes to feathers giving scaly appearance to back. Gregarious. Flight floppy on rounded black and white wings. Voice a characteristic 'pee-wit'. Breeds on fields, moorland and marshes. Winters on arable land, grassland, estuaries. Common.

Waders

Ringed Plover *Charadrius hiaticula* 20cm Small, fast-running plover. Adult sandy-brown above, white below. Face patterned black and white; black collar. Beak stubby, yellowish with black tip. Legs yellow. Immature has brownish markings, not black, and an incomplete collar. Rarely seen in large flocks. In flight, white wingbar conspicuous. Voice a fluting 'too-lee'; trilling song. Inhabits sandy coasts and salt pans, occasionally found inland on river banks and excavations. Widespread, relatively common.

Knot *Calidris canutus* 25cm Medium-small, often nondescript wader. Summer adult brown above, with golden scaly markings; underparts distinctly rusty red. Winter adult and immature nondescript, flecked grey-brown above, whitish below. Beak dark, straight, medium length. Legs dark, medium length. Gregarious, often gathering in close-packed flocks, thousands strong. In flight, faint white wingbar visible. Rarely vocal, occasional grunting calls. Breeds on Arctic tundra, winters on extensive sand and mudflats of sheltered coastal bays and estuaries. Widespread, locally very numerous.

Golden Plover *Pluvialis apricaria*
28cm Medium-sized plover.
Summer adult striking, with
richly-flecked golden crown,
nape and back separated from
glossy black face, throat and
belly by broad white margin.
Beak stubby. Legs grey, long.
Winter adult and immature
flecked dull golden-buff
above; underparts buff
shading to white on belly,
with no black. Often
gregarious. In flight, no
wingbar visible. Call a fluting
whistle 'tloo-ee'. Breeds on
tundra and moorland; winters
on coastal marshes and inland
on damp fields and grassland.
Locally common, sometimes in
large flocks.

Grey Plover *Pluvialis squatarola*
28cm Medium-sized, often
solitary plover. Summer adult
strikingly handsome:
upperparts silver-grey, richly
black-flecked, separated from
black face, throat, breast and
belly by broad white margin.
Winter adult and immature
flecked grey-buff above, white
below. Beak black, stubby.
Legs black, long. In flight,
shows a faint wingbar and
characteristic bold black
patches in 'armpits' beneath
wings. Call a plaintive, fluting
'tee-too-ee'. Breeds on
northern tundra. Winters on
sheltered coastal bays and
estuaries. Widespread, though
rarely numerous.

Waders

Turnstone *Arenaria interpres*
23cm Small, dumpy, harlequin-like wader. Summer adult has rich pale chestnut back; underparts, head and neck white, all boldly patterned with black. Winter adult and immature retain pied parts of plumage, but chestnut is replaced with grey. Beak dark, short, flattened from top to bottom; used to overturn weeds and stones. Legs yellowish. Feeds among seaweeds on rocky shores and is well camouflaged. In flight, white wingbars and pied plumage unmistakable. Staccato chattering 'tuk-uk-tuk' call. Breeds on tundra and rocky Arctic coasts. Winters on rocky coasts, rare inland. Widespread, often common.

Common Sandpiper *Actitis hypoleucos* 20cm Small wader. Summer adult sandy-brown above, flecked with white. Underparts mostly white; brown streaking on throat and on sides of breast forms a half collar. Winter adult and immature duller, less spotted. Beak dark, short and straight. Legs greenish. Bobs incessantly. Flight low over surface and fast; rapid, shallow wingbeats with wings downcurved; shows white wingbar, brown rump, brown tail with brown-barred white outer feathers. Trilling 'twee-wee-wee. . .' call. Song a high-pitched, rapid 'tittyweety-tittyweety'. Breeds beside lakes, rivers. Winters on marshes and coasts. Widespread, rarely numerous.

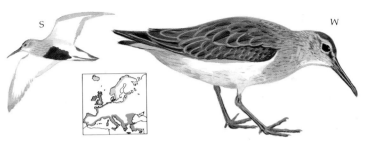

Dunlin *Calidris alpina* 18cm
Small wader. Summer adult
rich bronze with darker
rufous-brown speckling
above; breast pale, dark-
streaked; belly-patch black.
Winter adult and immature
dull speckled grey-brown or
buffish-brown above,
underparts paling to near-
white. Beak dark, relatively
long, slightly downcurved.
Legs dark, shortish.
Gregarious. In flight shows
pale wingbar and white
patches on each side of dark
rump and tail. Call a nasal
'treeer'; song a purring trill
delivered in flight. Breeds on
grassland, moorland and
tundra. At other times on
sheltered coastal bays,
estuaries, marshes and swamps.
Widespread, common.

Woodcock *Scolopax rusticola*
35cm Medium-large woodland
wader. Adult and immature
snipe-like, but heavier, with
bolder barring and finer
mottling on rich brown
plumage. Breast grey-buff,
barred. Head angular; *crosswise*
yellowish bands on rich brown
crown. Eyes large, bulging.
Beak yellowish-brown, long,
stout. Legs pinkish; short and
stout; squat stance. Rarely
flies until threatened. During
winter and spring displays
establishes 'roding' flight-
paths through woodland
glades. During display, voice a
frog-like 'orrrt-orrrt' with
high-pitched, sneezing 'swick'
calls, otherwise silent. Prefers
damp woodland; rare on fresh
or coastal marshes. Widespread
but difficult to see.

47

Waders

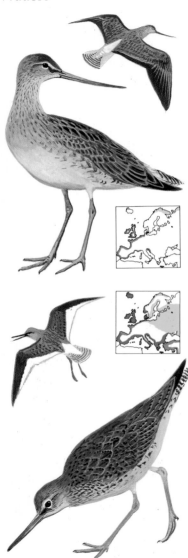

Bar-tailed Godwit *Limosa lapponica* 40cm Large, long-beaked wader. Summer adult richly marked brown on back; head, neck and breast rufous cinnamon-brown, belly chestnut. Winter adult and immature mottled grey to grey-brown above, shading to white below. Beak reddish, darker towards tip; very long, slightly upturned. Legs black and long. Gregarious, sometimes in large flocks. In flight shows dense, narrow, dark brown barring across white tail. Rarely vocal except in breeding season; usually a harsh 'kirrick'. Breeds on Arctic tundra. Winters on muddy or sandy estuaries or sheltered coastal bays. Common, locally numerous.

Redshank *Tringa totanus* 28cm Medium-sized wader. Summer adult rich brown above with pale flecks and fine dark brown streaks; buff below with heavy brown streaking; belly white. Winter adult and immature grey-brown above, grey-buff below, white on lower breast, belly and flanks. Beak reddish, slim, medium-long. Legs bright red, comparatively long. Occasionally gregarious. Wary. In flight, white wingbar, white rump and dark-barred white tail distinctive. Vocal; piping calls, usually variants of 'tu-lee-lee'. Breeds on marshes, wet meadows and moorland. Winters more often on salt marshes than fresh, and on estuaries and sandy bays.

Greenshank *Tringa nebularia*
30cm Medium-sized wader.
Summer adult grey-brown
above, richly flecked with
black and silver. Underparts
white. Winter adult and
immature paler and drabber
grey. Beak greenish, medium-
long, relatively stout, slightly
upturned. Legs green, long,
relatively stout. Rarely
gregarious. In flight, shows
all-dark wings and striking
white rump extending well up
back; tail white with dark
brown barring. Call a far-
carrying trisyllabic 'tu-tu-tu'.
Breeds on damp moorland,
marshes and tundra. On
migration and in winter
occasionally on fresh marshes,
more often on coastal lagoons
and sheltered sandy or muddy
estuaries and bays.

Curlew *Numenius arquata* 58cm
Very large wader. Adult and
immature sandy-buff above,
with whitish and brown flecks
and streaks. Underparts pale
buffish-fawn with darker
brown streaks, shading to
white on belly. Beak
brownish-black, exceptionally
long, markedly downcurved.
Legs blue-grey, relatively
long. Often gregarious in
winter. In flight, shows white
rump extending well up back,
and dark-barred buff tail.
Characteristic 'coor-lee' calls
at all times; in breeding season
has song flight with bubbling
trills. Breeds on moorland,
marshes and wet meadows.
Winters on sandy or muddy
coasts and estuaries.
Widespread, often common.

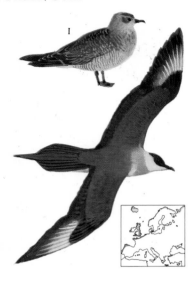

Arctic Skua *Stercorarius parasiticus* 45cm Medium-sized skua. Adults occur in two colour forms: dark phase uniformly chocolate-brown; pale phase sandy-brown above, cap blackish, neck, breast and belly buffish-white. Adult has slim elongated central tail feathers. Beak and legs greyish-brown, gull-like. Immature rich brown, heavily speckled and barred, lacks long tail feathers. In flight, shows white patches in long slender wings. Pursues other birds to steal food. Voice a yelping 'tuk-tuk', harsh 'eee-air'. Breeds colonially on moorland, remote islands, tundra. On migration in inshore waters. Regular; rarely numerous, except on breeding grounds.

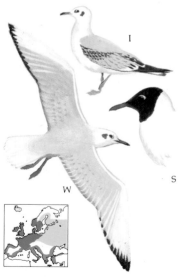

Black-headed Gull *Larus ridibundus* 35cm Medium-sized gull. Summer adult largely white, with chocolate hood. Wings pale silver-grey, black-tipped white flight feathers and white leading edge, characteristic in flight. Beak and legs blood-red. Winter adult lacks brown hood, has greyish nape and smudge through eye; beak and legs brownish. Immature wings have brownish bars on inner portion; black terminal band on white tail visible in flight. Gregarious. Various yelping 'keer' and drawn-out 'kwaar' calls. Breeds colonially on dunes, islands, marshes. In winter, almost ubiquitous coastally and inland, excluding mountainous regions. Common, often abundant.

Lesser Black-backed Gull
Larus fuscus 53cm Medium-large
gull. Adult predominantly
white; back and wings slate
grey; wingtips black with
small white markings. Beak
yellow, with red spot near tip.
Legs characteristically yellow.
Immature mottled brown and
white above, whitish below,
often impossible to distinguish
from young Herring.

Gregarious. Voice a powerful
'kay-ow', various laughing
'yah' calls and mewings.
Breeds (often in huge
colonies) on cliff tops, islands,
sand dunes and moorland
remote from human
disturbance. Migrates
southwards in winter to
coastal and inland habitats,
including urban areas.
Widespread, often common.

Herring Gull *Larus argentatus*
55cm Medium-sized gull.
Adult predominantly white;
back and wings silver-grey.
Wingtips black with white
markings. Beak yellow, with
red spot near tip. Legs pink;
yellow in southern and south-
western races. Immature
mottled brown and white
above, largely white below;
beak and legs brownish (*see*

Lesser Black-backed).
Gregarious. Vocal, with
various mewing cries, harsh
'kay-ow' and 'yah-yah-yah'
laughing calls. Breeds on
remote islands, moors, sand
dunes, cliffs and also
increasingly on buildings.
Winters in widespread
habitats from coasts to inland
and urban areas. Common,
often very numerous.

51

Gulls

Great Black-backed Gull *Larus marinus* 68cm Largest European gull. Adult largely white, jet black back and wings. Beak yellow with red spot near tip; large and strong. Legs pale pink. Immature speckled brown and white, tail white with broad black terminal bar. Takes four years to reach adult plumage. Flight powerful, wings showing conspicuous white trailing edge and white spots near tips of flight feathers. Voice a gruff 'kow-kow-kow'. Breeds on coastal islands and cliffs. The most maritime of large gulls, often wintering at sea, but also in coastal waters and inland, especially near refuse tips. Widespread.

Common Gull *Larus canus* 40cm Medium-sized gull. Adult predominantly white, occasionally with grey flecks around head and nape. Wings grey above; conspicuous black-and-white tips to flight feathers. Beak and legs greenish-yellow. Immature pale brown above, whitish below, with crown and nape streaked grey-brown; tail white with broad black terminal band; beak and legs dark brown. Gregarious. High-pitched 'kee-you' and 'gah-gah-gah' calls. Breeds on remote hillsides, islands, moorlands and tundra. Widespread on migration and in winter on farmland, grassland, urban areas, reservoirs and coasts of all types. Often common.

Kittiwake *Rissa tridactyla* 40cm
Medium-sized, slim-winged
gull. Adult largely white.
Wings pale grey; tips of flight
feathers black with no white
patches. Beak lemon yellow
with vermilion gape visible at
close range; small. Legs
distinctively black. Immature
similar, but with blackish
collar, black 'M' markings
across wings and black-tipped,
shallowly forked tail visible in
flight. Gregarious. Flight
buoyant and tern-like; wings
characteristically long and
slender. Very vocal at colony,
distinctive 'kitti-waaake' calls.
Breeds colonially on sea cliffs,
occasionally buildings. In
winter, most are well out to
sea, some remain in inshore
waters. Widespread, locally
numerous.

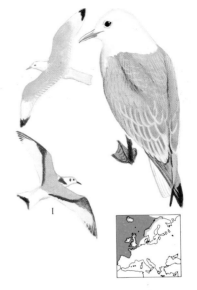

Black Tern *Chlidonias niger*
25cm Small, dark, marsh tern.
Summer adult largely dark
sooty-grey above and below;
tail dark grey, shallowly
forked. Head, breast and belly
jet black. Beak and legs black.
Winter adult grey above,
white below, with dark crown,
white forehead, and black
'half-collar' marks on
shoulders. Immature similar
to winter adult but browner.
Gregarious. Flight
characteristic, dipping down
to water surface to feed.
Rarely vocal, gives occasional
'krit' or 'kreek'. Breeds
colonially on swamps and
marshes. On migration seen
coastally and frequently
inland. Regular, locally
common.

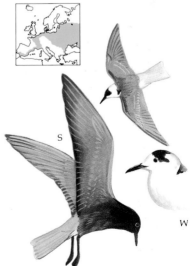

Terns

Common Tern *Sterna hirundo*
35cm Medium-sized sea tern.
Summer adult predominantly
white, with black cap. Wings
grey with appreciably darker
tips (*see* Arctic). Tail white,
deeply forked. Beak red with
black tip. Legs red. Winter
adult has white forehead.
Immature darker, with sandy-
grey markings on back and
wings. Gregarious. Voice a
harsh 'kee-aarh' with
emphasis on second syllable;
also hurried 'kirri-kirri-kirri'.
Breeds colonially on coastal
beaches and islands, and
increasingly often inland on
sand or gravel beside fresh
water. Feeds over coastal
lagoons, inshore waters and
various inland fresh waters
especially on migration.
Common.

Arctic Tern *Sterna paradisaea*
37cm Medium-sized sea tern.
Summer adult predominantly
white, with black cap. Wings
grey, distinctively pale and
translucent near tips. Tail
white, with long streamers.
Beak entirely red (*see*
Common). Legs red, very
short. Winter adult has white
forehead; beak and legs dark.
Immature similar, but with
sandy-brown back and wing
markings. Gregarious. Voice a
short, sharp 'keee-ah' with
emphasis on the first syllable.
Breeds colonially on remote
beaches, islands and grassy
areas near the sea. Feeds at
sea. On migration only
occasionally seen inland.
Widespread, locally common.

Guillemot *Uria aalge* 40cm
Medium-sized auk. Summer
adult chocolate-brown above
(northern birds almost black),
white below. Some ('bridled'
form), commoner in north,
have white eye-ring and stripe
behind eye. Beak long, dagger-
shaped. Legs grey. Winter
adult and immature similar
but grey, not brown. Long
and low-bodied while
swimming, stance upright on
cliffs. Dives frequently.
Gregarious. Whirring flight
low over sea, shows white
trailing edge to wing. Vocal
during breeding season with
various cooing and mooing
calls. Breeds colonially on sea
cliff ledges, winters in coastal
seas. Locally common.

Puffin *Fratercula arctica* 30cm
Medium-sized auk. Summer
adult unmistakable, black
above, white below, with large
white face-patch and huge
parrot-like beak striped grey-
blue, yellow and red. Legs and
feet bright orange-red. Winter
adult and immature drabber;
face-patch smoky-grey; beak
dark and much smaller.
Gregarious. Flight whirring
low over sea; characteristically
lacks white wingbar. Voice a
low growl in breeding season.
Breeds on sea coast cliffs,
screes and cliff-top grassland,
often in large colonies. Most
winter out at sea, some
remain inshore. Locally
common.

Woodpigeon *Columba palumbus* 40cm Large cumbersome pigeon. Adult and immature delicate grey-brown above, paler dove-grey below. Adult has metallic sheen on nape and conspicuous white collar-patches which are lacking in immature. Beak dark pink, short. Legs pinkish. Gregarious. In flight white crescentic wingbars are striking and diagnostic. Flight fast but clumsy. Voice a distinctive 'coo-*coo*-coo, coo-coo'. Breeds in woodland and scrub, feeds in woodland, on all types of farmland and in urban areas. Widespread, often common.

Stock Dove *Columba oenas* 33cm Medium-sized, farmland pigeon. Adult and immature uniformly dull leaden grey both above and below. Adults have a greenish metallic sheen on nape and pinkish flush to breast. Beak dark and short. Legs reddish. Gregarious. Flight swift and direct, showing distinctive black border to wing, two indistinct and irregular black wingbars, grey rump. Voice a booming 'coo-ooh', particularly in spring. Nests in holes on farmland and woodland, occasionally on coasts. Widespread, locally common.

Collared Dove *Streptopelia decaocto* 28cm Medium-small, sandy-coloured pigeon. Adult and immature sandy-brown on back and wings. Head, neck, breast and belly appreciably paler pinkish-buff. Collar-band a black and white continuous crescent, distinctive in adult, lacking in immature. Gregarious. In flight, wings show dark tips and conspicuous blue-grey forewing patches; brown tail with broad, white terminal band is striking. Voice a dry 'aaah' in flight; also strident 'coo-*coo*-coo'. Inhabits farmland, parks, urban areas. Widespread and common.

Turtle Dove *Streptopelia turtur* 28cm Medium-small pigeon. Adult rich bronze; back and wings mottled with brown and black. Underparts pinkish-buff shading to white on belly. Head and neck grey with chequered black and white collar-patches. Wings dark tipped; tail blackish with diagnostic narrow white border visible in flight (*see* Collared). Immature duller and browner, lacking collars. Gregarious. Flight swift and direct. Voice a distinctive and prolonged purring. Inhabits woodland, farmland with hedges, scrub. Widespread, fairly common.

Owls

Tawny Owl *Strix aluco* 38cm
Medium-sized, round-headed owl. Adult and immature brown above, quite frequently rich chestnut, occasionally almost grey, with fine black streaks and bold buff blotches. Underparts buffish-brown, finely marked with darker brown. Head large, conspicuously rounded. Facial disc roughly circular, grey-buff with narrow black border. Eyes all-dark, large. Nocturnal hunter; secretive during day when whereabouts are often revealed by flocks of agitated small birds. In flight, markedly round-winged. Voice the well-known, tremulous 'hoo-hoo-hoooo' and sharp 'kew-wit'. Inhabits woodland, farmland, urban areas. Widespread.

Little Owl *Athene noctua* 23cm
Small, bold owl, often seen in daylight. Adult and immature grey-brown above, with bold white spots and streaks. Underparts whitish or greyish-buff, heavily streaked with dark brown. Head comparatively large, flat-crowned. Facial disc oblong, greyish with paler margin; eyes bright yellow with dark pupils. Stance squat but upright, often perches on post and bobs occasionally if approached. Flight undulating on short, conspicuously rounded wings. Hunts during the evening and at night. Various puppy-like yelps, and a penetrating 'poo-oop'. Habitat widely varied. Widespread, locally fairly common.

Barn Owl *Tyto alba* 35cm Pale, medium-sized owl. Adult and immature pale sandy-brown above, delicately flecked with brown, grey and white. Underparts white in birds from north-western Europe, including Britain and Ireland, or rich buff, even chestnut, in birds from western and southern Europe. Facial disc white, heart-shaped. Eyes dark brown, large. Stance upright, legs long and 'knock-kneed'. Usually nocturnal, but in winter may hunt in daylight. In flight, relatively long wings appear very pale. Various snoring noises when roosting, occasional strident shriek at other times. Inhabits open woodland, farmland, heaths, villages. Widespread, nowhere numerous.

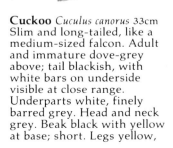

Cuckoo *Cuculus canorus* 33cm Slim and long-tailed, like a medium-sized falcon. Adult and immature dove-grey above; tail blackish, with white bars on underside visible at close range. Underparts white, finely barred grey. Head and neck grey. Beak black with yellow at base; short. Legs yellow, short. Rare rufous form (female and immature only) has rich brown upperparts. Voice a characteristic 'cuck-oo' and variants; female has bubbling trill and male rasping chuckle. Inhabits woodland, farmland, heath, scrub, moorland and marshes. Widespread, often numerous.

Kingfisher *Alcedo atthis* 17cm
Small but unmistakable. Adult
upperparts electric blue-green;
crown dark blue with paler
blue flecks. Cheeks chestnut
and white. Underparts bright
chestnut. Immature slightly
duller, with heavily flecked
crown. Beak all-black or
showing some red at base;
long, dagger-shaped. Legs and
feet bright scarlet and tiny.
Silhouette dumpy with
oversize beak and head. Flight
arrow-like on whirring wings
low over water. Voice a shrill
ringing 'cheet'. Inhabits lakes,
rivers and streams,
occasionally coasts in winter.
Widespread.

Hoopoe *Upupa epops* 28cm
Medium-sized, with fawn and
pied plumage. Adult and
immature have back and
wings boldly barred black and
white, tail black with white
bar. Head, neck and breast
unusual and characteristic
pinkish sandy-fawn; belly
white. Long, black-tipped, pale
ginger crest on head, erected
into fan when excited or
alarmed. Beak dark, long,
slender and downcurved. Legs
short. Flight characteristically
flopping. Voice a far-carrying
repetitive 'poo-poo-poo'.
Inhabits open country with
trees and scrub, orchards,
olive groves. Widespread, but
rarely numerous.

Great Spotted Woodpecker
Dendrocopos major 23cm Smallish
pied woodpecker. Adult
upperparts barred boldly in
black and white; underparts
whitish, with extensive area
of red beneath tail. Forehead
white; crown and neck black
(with scarlet nape-patch in
male only); white cheeks and
patches on sides of neck. Beak
black, short and stout.
Immature greyer; crown and
tail scarlet. Flight undulating,
showing bold barring across
back and striking white wing-
patches. Voice an explosive
'kek' or 'chack'. Drums often.
Inhabits all types of woodland,
urban parks and gardens,
farmland with large trees.
Widespread, often common.

Green Woodpecker *Picus viridis*
30cm Medium-sized
woodpecker. Adult strikingly
green and gold above,
greenish-grey below with
darker barring on flanks.
Crown and nape red in both
sexes, striking moustachial
streaks red and black in male,
black in female. Beak grey
with black tip, relatively long.
Immature paler; crown
reddish, upperparts heavily
buff-spotted; breast and
flanks barred. Often feeds on
ground. Flight deeply
undulating, gold rump
conspicuous. Voice a
characteristic ringing laugh,
'yah-yah-yah'; drums
relatively rarely. Inhabits open
dry grassland, heath, scrub
and deciduous woodland.
Widespread.

61

Swallow *Hirundo rustica* 20cm
Typical small hirundine. Adult
and immature dark glossy
blue-black over much of the
upperparts; underparts
predominantly white. Face-
patch dark chestnut. In flight,
shows slender curved wings,
slim silhouette and long,
deeply forked tail with narrow
streamers, longer in adults
than immatures and longer in
males than females; white
spots on tail conspicuous.
Flight swift, swooping; feeds
on the wing. Voice a
prolonged musical twittering,
call a sharp 'chirrup'. Breeds in
buildings on farmland and in
urban areas, feeds over most
habitats. Common.

House Martin *Delichon urbica*
12cm Tiny, pied hirundine.
Adult glossy blue-black on
upperparts, with rather duller,
blackish flight feathers and
diagnostic bold white rump-
patch. Tail blue-black,
shallowly forked. Underparts
white. Legs and toes white
and feathered, visible when
collecting mud for nest.
Immature greyer and lacking
iridescent sheen. Gregarious.
Voice an unmusical rattling
twitter. Nests colonially on
buildings, often in towns,
occasionally on cliffs; feeds
over open land and fresh
waters. Widespread, often
numerous.

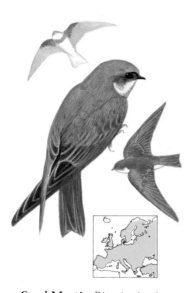

Sand Martin *Riparia riparia*
12cm Tiny hirundine. Adult
and immature sandy-brown
above, whitish below with
characteristic brown band
across breast. Tail brown,
short, shallowly forked. Beak
and legs black, tiny. Eyes
relatively large. Immature has
pale feather fringes giving
scaly appearance. Gregarious.
Spends much of its time on
the wing. Voice a soft rattling
trill; sharp chirrup alarm call.
Breeds colonially in sandy
banks, often feeds by hawking
over nearby fresh waters.
Widespread, locally numerous.

Swift *Apus apus* 18cm Small,
with characteristic sickle-
shaped wings. Adult sooty-
black above and below, save
for greyish-white throat
visible at close range. Tail
short, shallowly forked. Beak
and legs tiny; eyes large and
dark. Immature dull grey,
with pale grey scaly markings.
Often gregarious. Flight fast
and characteristically
flickering; wings distinctively
long and narrow. Highly
mobile bird spending much of
its life on the wing. Shrill,
very high-pitched scream.
Breeds colonially in urban
areas, feeds over almost any
habitat. Widespread, locally
numerous.

Larks

Skylark *Alauda arvensis* 18cm
Typical lark. Adult and
immature buffish-brown
above, richer chestnut-brown
on wings and back, all
feathers with dark centres and
pale fringes; flight feathers
blackish. Underparts pale buff,
heavily streaked brown on
breast. Head pale buff, dark
brown streaks; short crest
raised when excited. Eyestripe
pale buff extending as pale
margin to cheek-patch. Beak
pale brown, stout. Legs
pinkish-brown. In flight,
white trailing edge to blackish
tail visible. Call a liquid
'chirrup'; song musical
produced in flight high above
ground. Inhabits open
farmland, marshes, moors,
heaths, mountains. Often
abundant.

Crested Lark *Galerida cristata*
17cm Typical lark with striking
crest. Adult and immature
rich fawn on upperparts,
tinged chestnut and with
brown streaking. Underparts
pale buffish-white; throat and
breast finely streaked with
dark brown. Crest on crown
brown, dark-streaked, long,
often held erect. Beak
brownish, relatively long.
Legs pale brown. In flight,
brown tail with striking,
sandy-chestnut outer feathers
is characteristic. Call 'doo-dee-
doo'; song similar to Skylark
but usually produced from
ground. Inhabits open land,
farms, roadside verges, often
near towns. Common,
though, strangely, extremely
rare in Britain and Ireland.

Meadow Pipit *Anthus pratensis*
15cm Small, nondescript pipit.
Adult and immature brownish
above (shade varying from
yellowish, through olive to
greenish) with abundant
darker streaks. Underparts
pale grey-buff, shading to
white on belly, with dark
streaks on breast and flanks.
Legs dark brown. Call a thin
'seep'; song (often produced in
parachuting song-flight) a
weak descending trill (see
Tree). Inhabits open
moorland, heath, farmland
and marshes. Widespread,
often common.

Tree Pipit *Anthus trivialis* 15cm
Predominantly woodland
pipit. Adult and immature
have upperparts of rich
yellow-brown with plentiful,
fine, darker brown streaks.
Breast buff, shading to white
on belly; conspicuous dark
brown streaks on breast and
flanks. Rather stockier in
build than Meadow, and with
pinkish legs. Call a distinctive
'tee-zee'; song, usually
produced in parachuting
display flight, a characteristic
descending trill ending in a
series of 'see-aah' notes.
Inhabits woodland clearings
and heathland with trees.
Widespread, locally common.

Pipits and Wagtails

Rock Pipit *Anthus petrosa* 17cm
Largish, dark pipit. Adult and
immature largely brownish-
grey above, with plentiful
darker streaks, and pale grey-
buff below with heavy, dark
brown markings. Tail long
and dark, with characteristic
smoky-grey outer tail
feathers. Legs grey, relatively
long. Continental Water Pipit
is similar but paler. Call a
strident 'zeep'; song a strong
descending trill, often
produced in a parachuting
display flight. Frequents rocky
coastlines. Widespread, but
not numerous.

Yellow Wagtail *Motacilla flava
flavissima* 17cm Comparatively
short-tailed wagtail. Summer
adult male has upperparts
olive-green, some yellow on
nape; underparts rich canary
yellow. Eyestripe yellow,
separating greenish crown
from darker cheek-patch. Tail
black, white edges. Summer
female brownish-olive above,
buff shading on breast and
flanks; underparts paler
yellow, throat and breast near
white. Winter adults duller,
resembling immature, which
is grey-brown above, with
whitish eyestripe over dark
cheek-patch, pale buff below,
only trace of yellow undertail.
Often gregarious. Call a rich
'tseep'; song musical. Inhabits
meadows, farmland and
marshes. Locally common.

Grey Wagtail *Motacilla cinerea*
18cm Longest-tailed of the
European wagtails. Summer
adult male has upperparts
dove-grey, with bold white
eyestripe separating grey
crown from darker cheeks.
Tail black with white outer
feathers; long. Underparts
lemon-yellow, particularly
rich beneath tail. Summer
male has white moustachial
streaks and black bib absent in
winter. Female and immature
duller; breast whitish yellow
confined to undertail. Call a
high-pitched 'chee-seek'; song
resembles Blue Tit, 'tsee-tsee-
tsee' followed by trill.
Frequents fast-moving
watersides: streams, rapids,
sluices. Widespread.

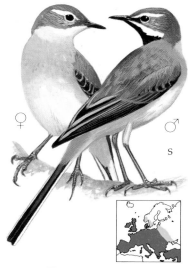

White Wagtail *Motacilla alba
alba* 18cm Typical pied plumage
wagtail of continental Europe.
Summer adult male silvery-
grey on back; forehead white,
nape black. Cheeks white,
throat and breast black, rest
of underparts white. Summer
female similar but duller.
Winter adults and immature
have grey backs, smoky napes,
white faces and throats, grey
moustachial stripes and
indistinct blackish collar. Call
a soft disyllabic 'swee-eep';
twittering song. Inhabits open
grassland and waterside in
farmland and urban areas.
Common.

Dunnock *Prunella modularis*
15cm Small and drab. Adult
has dark brown upperparts
with prominent darker
markings. Head, nape and
breast are distinctive leaden
grey, belly buff. Immature
browner, lacking grey,
conspicuously pale-speckled
above. Spends much time on
ground, hopping under
vegetation, often flicking tail.
Call a shrill 'seek', often loud
in evening; song a brief,
suddenly-interrupted,
melodious warble. Inhabits
woodland of all types,
farmland, scrub, town parks
and gardens. Widespread,
locally common.

Dipper *Cinclus cinclus* 17cm
Dumpy, like a thrush-sized
Wren. Adult has rich, dark
brown upperparts. Throat and
breast strikingly white; belly
rich chestnut (Britain and
Ireland) or blackish (rest of
Europe). Immature scaly grey,
darker above than below.
Characteristically stands,
bobbing, on rocks before
plunging into river. Flight
fast, whirring and low over
water. Call a loud 'zit'; song a
fragmented warbling.
Frequents fast-flowing clear
rivers in hilly country,
occasionally lakes or sheltered
coasts. Locally common.

Wren *Troglodytes troglodytes* 10cm
One of the smallest European
birds. Adult and immature
rich chestnut-brown above,
barred with dark brown;
underparts rather paler with
less barring. Tail
characteristically narrow and
carried cocked upright. Spends
much time on ground under
dense vegetation. Flight low
and direct on short, rounded
whirring wings. Call a
scolding 'churr'; song musical,
extended and astonishingly
loud. Well vegetated habitats
of all types, also cliffs and
mountain screes. Widespread,
often common.

Robin *Erithacus rubecula* 13cm
Small but well known. Adult
predominantly sandy-brown
above; face, throat and breast
orange-red, broadly edged
with dark grey. Grey on lower
breast is extensive, shading to
white on belly. Wingbars buff,
narrow; conspicuous in
perched bird, not striking in
flight. Tail sandy-brown,
unmarked. Immature darker
brown above, pale buff below,
copiously speckled and barred.
Call a sharp 'tick'; song a high-
pitched warble. Inhabits
woods, parks and urban
gardens, usually with plentiful
undergrowth. Widespread and
common.

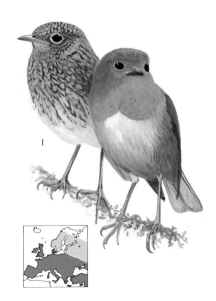

Thrushes and Chats

Black Redstart *Phoenicurus ochruros* 15cm Small, very dark chat. Summer adult male dark ash-grey above. Rump and tail (often flicked) conspicuously chestnut-red. White wingbar striking, especially in older birds. Face and breast sooty-black, belly white. Winter plumage duller, retains chestnut tail. Female uniformly drab, dark grey-brown, but tail characteristic chestnut-red. Immature dark brown with copious paler spots, tail chestnut. Call a sharp 'tick'; song a rapid, but brief, rattling warble. Inhabits mountain screes and towns, including large factory sites. Widespread, locally common.

Redstart *Phoenicurus phoenicurus* 15cm Small, red-tailed chat. Summer adult male unmistakable, upperparts strikingly pale blue-grey, forehead white, tail chestnut. Face and throat black, breast bright chestnut, belly white. Plumage altogether browner and less well-marked in winter. Female brown above, fawn below, tail chestnut. Immature brown, paler below, copiously buff-flecked like immature Robin but tail chestnut, paler and shorter than tail of immature Nightingale. Call a melodious 'tu-eet'; song a brief melodious warble ending in a dry rattle. Inhabits woodlands of all descriptions, sometimes scrub. Widespread, locally common.

Stonechat *Saxicola torquata* 13cm
Small, upright and noisy chat.
Summer adult male has dark
brown back, white rump and
black tail. Head and throat
black; neck patches white.
Breast orange-buff, shading
towards white on belly.
Winter plumage similar, but
obscured by pale feather
fringes. Female similarly
patterned, browner and
heavily streaked; lacking
white rump. Immature brown
above, paler below, copiously
buff speckled. Frequently
perches on bushes, wings and
tail flicking. Call a sharp
'tcchack'; song a high-pitched
scratchy warble, often
produced in song flight.
Inhabits heath and scrub,
inland or coastal. Widespread,
locally common.

Whinchat *Saxicola rubetra* 13cm
Small, upright chat. Summer
adult male speckled brown
and fawn above, with bold
white eyestripe separating
crown from characteristic
dark cheek-patch. Tail dark
brown with distinctive white
markings at base visible in
flight. Underparts pale
orange. Winter plumage
appreciably duller. Female
paler and duller than male.
Immature paler and duller;
underparts heavily streaked.
Often perches on low bushes
or tufts of grass. Wings and
tail constantly flicked. Call a
harsh 'teck'; song a short,
high-pitched warble, often
produced in song-flight.
Inhabits open grassland, heath
and scrub. Widespread but
only locally numerous.

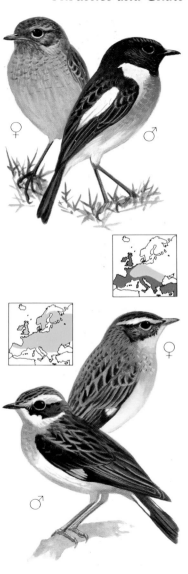

Thrushes and Chats

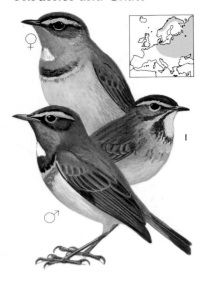

Bluethroat *Luscinia svecica* 15cm
Small, secretive thrush.
Summer adult male brown
above; characteristic chestnut
patches on each side of base of
tail often striking as it dives
for cover. Throat and breast
bright blue fringed with black
and chestnut, with white
central spot (southern race) or
red (northern race). Breast
colours duller but still
distinctive at other seasons.
Female has white throat
fringed with black. Immature
resembles slim, immature
Robin but has chestnut tail
markings. Call a sharp 'tack';
song an extended high-pitched
melodious warble. Inhabits
northern swampy scrub or
heathland. Locally fairly
common.

Black-eared Wheatear
Oenanthe hispanica 15cm Small,
terrestrial chat. Adult male
pale cinnamon brown above
and below; wings black. Two
forms occur: one with a large
black patch through the eye,
the other with a complete
black face and throat. Winter
plumage appreciably duller.
Female and immature similar
to Wheatear, but with darker
cheeks and wings. In flight,
characteristic white inverted
'V' marking on rump and tail
prominent. Call a harsh
'tchack'; song a high-pitched,
scratchy warble. Inhabits dry,
open, often stony areas with
mostly low-growing
vegetation. Locally common.

Wheatear *Oenanthe oenanthe*
15cm Small, pale chat.
Summer adult male pale grey
above; underparts apricot-
buff. Wings blackish; tail
black, white inverted 'V' mark
on rump and base of tail
conspicuous in flight. Eye-
patch black. Winter plumage
browner. Female grey-brown
above, buff below; eye-patch
brown. Immature similar, but
buff-speckled. Both show
distinctive tail and rump
pattern. Largely terrestrial,
running in short bursts, then
pausing, tail cocked. Call a
harsh 'tack'; song a brief,
scratchy warble, often
produced in song flight.
Inhabits open areas of heath,
grassland or moorland, often
with scanty vegetation.
Widespread, locally common.

Blackbird *Turdus merula* 25cm
Familiar and comparatively
long tailed. Male plumage
unmistakable, entirely glossy
velvet black; beak and eye-
ring contrasting orange.
Female dark brown above,
paler below; throat whitish
with dark border; beak dark
with trace of yellow at base.

Immature rather more ginger-
brown than female, heavily
buff-spotted. Call a loud
'chink' or 'chack', often
persistent; song fluting,
varied, extended and
melodious. Inhabits farmland,
woodland, heaths and urban
areas. Widespread, often
abundant.

Thrushes and Chats

Mistle Thrush *Turdus viscivorus*
27cm Largish, pale and
relatively long-tailed thrush.
Adult pale grey-brown above;
underparts whitish, heavily
spotted with brown. Wings
dark brown. Tail long, dark
with pale grey-buff outer
feathers. Immature greyer,
appears much paler because of
copious, pale scaly feather
margins on upperparts. In
flight, characteristic white
underwing conspicuous. Call
an angry extended rattle; song
simple and slow but tuneful,
often produced early in spring
and usually delivered from a
prominent perch. Inhabits
woodland, parks, gardens and
well-treed farmland; often on
open grassland in winter.
Widespread.

Song Thrush *Turdus philomelos*
23cm Smallish, short-tailed,
upright thrush. Adult olive or
sandy-brown above, tinged
yellowish-buff, with pale
eyestripe above darker brown
cheek-patch. Wings and tail
chestnut-brown. Underparts
greyish-white, tinged
cinnamon, heavily streaked
with dark brown. Immature
similar, but with copious
yellow-buff speckling on
upperparts. In flight,
underwings are pale sandy-
brown (*see* Redwing, Mistle).
Call a thin 'seep'; song (often
from a prominent perch) a
series of musical notes, each
repeated two or three times.
Inhabits woods, parks,
gardens and farmland with
plentiful trees. Widespread,
often common.

Fieldfare *Turdus pilaris* 25cm
Comparatively long-tailed
thrush. Adult has back,
mantle and wings rich golden
russet-brown. Breast golden-
buff shading to white on belly,
heavily speckled. Crown, nape
and rump dove-grey,
contrasting with black tail.
Immature is browner above,
fawn below, heavily speckled.
Often gregarious. Call a very
characteristic series of
laughing 'chacks'; song a
scratchy warble. Breeds in
northern forests, parks and
gardens, winters on open
farmland and open woodland.
Widespread, often common.

Redwing *Turdus iliacus* 20cm
Smallish dark, short-tailed
thrush. Adult is dark russet-
brown above, with
conspicuous buffish eyestripe
and moustachial streak on
either edge of dark cheek-
patch. Underparts whitish,
streaked dark brown, with
conspicuous reddish flanks.
Immature similar but duller,
with copious sandy speckling
on back. In flight,
characteristic red underwing
is prominent. Often
gregarious. Call an extended
'see-eep'; song a low series of
fluting notes. Breeds in
northern forests, parks and
gardens, winters in woodland
and on open farmland,
occasionally in parks and
gardens. Widespread, often
numerous.

Nightingale *Luscinia megarhynchos* 17cm Small, drab thrush but an incomparable songster. Adult olive-brown above, with striking, long, round-ended rufous tail. Underparts pale buff, almost white on belly, always unmarked. Immature sandy-brown above, paler below, copiously spotted but with long rufous tail. Legs relatively long and strong, suited to terrestrial habits. Call a soft 'hoo-eet'; song long, loud and melodious, richly varied and containing some mimicry of other birds, often produced night and day. Inhabits dense woodland undergrowth and swampy thickets. Widespread, locally common.

Reed Warbler *Acrocephalus scirpaceus* 13cm Tiny, unstreaked warbler. Adult and immature have rich reddish-brown upperparts lacking darker streaks; tail reddish-brown, relatively long and tapered towards tip. Eyestripe faint buffish. Underparts whitish, shading to buff on flanks. Legs normally dark brown. Alarm call 'churr'; song prolonged and repetitive, with spells of chirruping, more musical and less twangy than Sedge, with some mimicry. Normally inhabits reedbeds, sometimes other heavily vegetated fresh water margins. Widespread, often common.

Cetti's Warbler *Cettia cetti* 15cm
Small, unstreaked warbler.
Adult and immature have
entire upperparts rich
reddish-brown, shading to
buff on sides of breast and
flanks, and to white on belly.
Tail rich brown, relatively
long, and conspicuously
rounded at the tip. Secretive,
normally flying only short
distance between clumps of
vegetation. Call a sharp 'teck';
song an explosive burst of
metallic 'cher-chink' notes.
Inhabits damp, heavily
vegetated marshes, ditches,
swamps and scrub. Non-
migratory. Widespread, locally
common.

Sedge Warbler *Acrocephalus
schoenobaenus* 13cm Tiny,
heavily-streaked warbler.
Adult and immature have
olive-brown back, heavily
streaked with blackish-brown;
tail brown, tinged chestnut.
Underparts whitish, tinged
buff on flanks. Crown brown,
with narrow blackish stripes,
separated by clear whitish
eyestripe from grey-brown
cheeks. Inquisitive, but rarely
flies far in the open. Call an
explosive 'tuck' of alarm; song
(often produced in short,
vertical song-flight) a rapid,
repetitive, metallic jingle,
often loud and interspersed
with chattering notes.
Inhabits reedbeds and adjacent
shrubby swamps. Widespread,
often common.

Warblers

Whitethroat *Sylvia communis*
14cm Small active warbler.
Adult male grey above, wings
characteristic pale chestnut,
tail dull brown with white
edge. Throat strikingly white,
rest of underparts whitish,
tinged pinkish-buff. Legs
brownish. Female and
immature browner and paler,
but with chestnut wings still
evident. Active but fairly
secretive, except in song. Call
a rasping 'tschack'; song a
rapid, scratchy warble, usually
produced in song-flight.
Inhabits heath, scrubby
hillsides, maquis and
woodland clearings.
Widespread, locally common.

Garden Warbler *Sylvia borin*
15cm Small warbler, lacking
distinctive features. Adult
characteristically drab
greyish-olive on upperparts;
underparts whitish shaded
grey or buff, especially on the
flanks. Head rounded, with
comparatively heavy beak.
Eyestripe faint and pale. Legs
bluish. Immature paler,
yellowish-buff. Secretive. Call
a sharp 'tack'; song an
extended, liquid, melodious
warbling, usually produced in
deep cover. Inhabits well-
grown, thick scrub or dense
woodland undergrowth; tall
trees seem unnecessary
(unlike Blackcap). Widespread,
occasionally quite common.

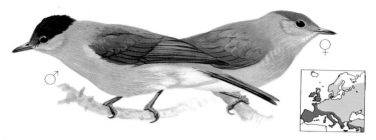

Blackcap *Sylvia atricapilla* 15cm
Small warbler. Adult male is
greyish-olive above, with
characteristic black crown;
underparts pale grey. Legs
bluish. Female and immature
have grey plumage with
browner tinge; cap brown in
female, ginger-chestnut in
immature. Call a sharp 'tack';
song a melodious warble,
similar to but briefer than
Garden Warbler, usually
ending in a rising note.
Inhabits parks, gardens and
woodland with both well-
developed undergrowth and
tall trees. Widespread, locally
quite common.

Wood Warbler *Phylloscopus
sibilatrix* 13cm Small, but one of
the larger leaf warblers. Adult
and immature have yellowish-
olive upperparts. Wings
brown, with yellowish feather
fringes but lacking wingbars.
Eyestripe yellowish, distinct;
face, throat and breast rich
yellow. Rest of underparts
strikingly white. Legs pale
pinkish-brown. Call a liquid
dee-you'; song a characteristic
trill based on an accelerating
repetition of 'sip' notes, often
produced in song-flight.
Inhabits mature deciduous
woodland, often with
comparatively little
undergrowth. Widespread,
locally common.

Warblers

Willow Warbler *Phylloscopus trochilus* 10cm Tiny leaf warbler. Adult and immature have pale olive-green upperparts, with a clear whitish eyestripe. Underparts are whitish, strongly tinged with yellow in immature, especially on the flanks. Legs usually brown (*see* Chiffchaff).

Call a plaintive 'too-eet'; song a characteristic, melodious and silvery descending warble with a final flourish. Inhabits woodlands with dense undergrowth, heath, parkland and, in the far north, scrub without trees. Widespread and common.

Chiffchaff *Phylloscopus collybita* 10cm Tiny, drab leaf warbler. Adult and immature have drab brownish-olive upperparts; wings brown lacking wingbars; tail brown. Eyestripe pale yellow. Underparts whitish, shaded buff on flanks, often yellow-tinged in immature. Legs

usually blackish. Call a plaintive 'hoo-eet'; song striking and diagnostic, a monotonous series of 'chiff' 'chaff' notes. Favours mature woodlands with both tall trees and well-developed undergrowth; rarely in scrub except on migration. Widespread, often common.

Firecrest *Regulus ignicapillus* 9cm
Smallest European bird. Adult
and immature have olive
green upperparts, tinged
golden-bronze on the mantle
in adults; wings brownish
with double white wingbars;
tail brown, short. Underparts
whitish. Head pattern (lacking
in immature) striking and
diagnostic, with crown stripe
orange (flame in male) edged
in black and contrasting with
bold white stripe over eye.
Call a rasping high-pitched
'tsee'; song a monotonous
accelerating repetition of 'tsee'
notes lacking final flourish of
Goldcrest. Inhabits woodland
of all types. Widespread,
locally common.

Goldcrest *Regulus regulus* 9cm
Tiny, one of the smallest
European birds. Adult and
immature have olive-green
upperparts; wings brownish
with double white wingbar;
tail brown, short. Underparts
whitish. Head pattern
characteristic, with crown-
stripe flame coloured in male,
yellowish-gold in female,
broadly edged in black; diffuse
white eye-ring. Beak dark,
short and finely pointed. Legs
dark brown. Immature lacks
head pattern. Call a very high-
pitched 'tsee'; song also high-
pitched, a descending series of
'tsee-tsee' notes terminating
in flourishing trill. Inhabits
woodland of all types,
occasionally parks and
gardens. Widespread and
common.

Flycatchers

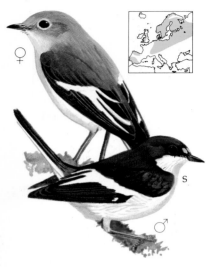

Pied Flycatcher *Ficedula hypoleuca* 13cm Small flycatcher with pied plumage. Summer adult male has black upperparts (year-old birds may have brownish wings and tail); wingbars bold white; forehead has white patch. Tail black with white edges, frequently flicked. Underparts white. Winter male, female and immature brown above, white below with grey-buff shading. Call a sharp 'wit'; song an unmelodious rattle of notes. Inhabits mature woodland, usually deciduous, with scant undergrowth. Locally common.

Spotted Flycatcher *Muscicapa striata* 15cm Small, elongated flycatcher. Adult and immature have drab brown upperparts with dark brown, closely-spaced streaks on crown. Underparts buff shading to white on belly; breast has brown streaking. Immature has scaly pale markings on back when freshly fledged. Flight characteristic, dashing out from prominent perch to catch insect prey, usually returning to same perch; shows relatively long wings and tail. Call a sharp 'zit'; song a brief sequence of squeaky notes. Inhabits woodland clearings, scrub, farmland, parks and gardens with plentiful trees. Widespread.

Long-tailed Tit *Aegithalos caudatus* 15cm Tiny but long-tailed. Adult and immature have fluffy body; upperparts largely white and brown, tinged pink; tail black, white edged. Underparts white, tinged pale buffish-pink on belly and flanks. Head white with dark stripes over eyes (head all-white in northern race); reddish, fleshy wattles over eyes. Beak black, short and stubby. Tends to move in noisy flocks. Flight feeble on short, rounded wings. Calls a repeated thin 'see', or a low 'tupp'; song (rarely heard) varied 'see' and 'tsew' notes. Inhabits woodland undergrowth, scrub, heathland and farmland hedges. Widespread, often common.

Bearded Tit *Panurus biarmicus* 15cm Small and long-tailed. Adult male predominantly chestnut-brown above. Tail long and relatively broad. Head distinctive dove-grey. Throat white, with characteristic, broad black moustachial streaks; rest of underparts pale buff. Female and immature brown above, cap darker; underparts grey-buff. Tends to move in flocks. Flight feeble on short, rounded wings. Call a distinctive 'ping'; song a twittering rattle. Inhabits wetlands with extensive *Phragmites* reed beds. Locally common.

Tits

Great Tit *Parus major* 15cm
Largest of the tits. Adult back
greenish; wings blue-grey
with white wingbars; tail
blackish with conspicuous
white edges. Crown and nape
glossy black, with striking
white cheeks and indistinct
whitish nape-patch. Breast
and belly yellow, with central
black stripe broader in male
than female. Immature duller
and greener, with grey-green
rather than black markings.
Feeds more often on ground
than other tits. Calls varied,
but 'tchink' common; song a
repetitive, ringing 'tea-cher,
tea-cher'. Inhabits woodland
of all types, farmland, parks
and gardens. Widespread,
often numerous.

Coal Tit *Parus ater* 12cm Tiny,
agile tit. Adult and immature
have olive-grey upperparts
(bluer in Continental birds).
Underparts pale buff, with
richer cinnamon tones on
flanks. Head and bib glossy
black (duller in immature)
relieved by contrasting white
patches on cheeks and nape.
Call a high-pitched, plaintive
'tseet'; song a repetitive, high-
pitched 'wheat-see, wheat-
see'. Inhabits woodland of all
types, but favours conifers;
also found in gardens and
parks. Widespread, often
common.

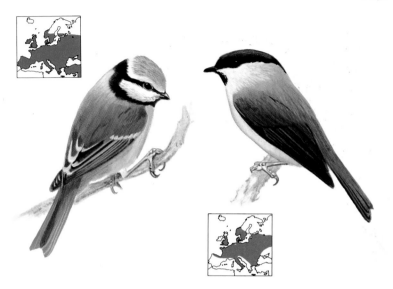

Blue Tit *Parus caeruleus* 12cm
Tiny tit. Adult has greenish
back; wings and tail
characteristic bright blue.
Underparts yellow. Head
white, with bright blue crown,
black line through eye and
black bib. Male shows brighter
blues than female. Immature
less well-marked, with
greenish upperparts and
lacking blue crown until
autumn. Varied calls, but
'tsee-tsee-tsee-sit' often used;
song a fast trill opening with a
series of 'tsee' notes. Habitat
ranges from woodland of all
types to urban gardens,
farmland and even marshland
in winter. Widespread, often
numerous.

Marsh Tit *Parus palustris* 13cm
Small, sombre brownish tit.
Adult and immature have
upperparts of uniform brown;
wings and tail slightly darker
brown. Crown and nape
glossy black, contrasting with
whitish cheeks. Underparts
largely greyish-buff, with
small black bib on throat. Call
a diagnostic, explosive 'pit-
chew'; song a bell-like note
repeated several times, or
sometimes 'pitchaweeoo'
variants of the call. Inhabits
woodland, usually deciduous
or mixed with abundant
undergrowth; scrub, park and
garden shrubberies.
Widespread but rarely
numerous.

Treecreeper *Certhia familiaris*
12cm Woodpecker-like but
tiny. Adult and immature
have dark brown upperparts,
densely streaked with white,
more conspicuously so in
immature. Tail brown, long,
central feathers pointed.
Underparts whitish, often
stained with green or brown
from tree trunks. Long
whitish eyestripe over darker
brown cheek-patch; eye large
and dark. Beak long and fairly
pointed, downcurved. Creeps
mouse-like, head-up on bark.
Flight deeply undulating,
showing multiple wingbars.
Call a shrill 'tseeu'; song a
high-pitched descending series
of notes with final flourish.
Inhabits mature woodland,
especially conifers. Widespread
but rarely numerous.

Nuthatch *Sitta europaea* 15cm
Small and woodpecker-like.
Adult and immature have
distinctive blue-grey
upperparts; wings dark grey;
tail feathers white-tipped,
dove-grey. Eyestripe broad
and black. Throat white, rest
of underparts pale buff,
shading to rich chestnut on
flanks of male, cinnamon on
female. Northern race almost
completely white below. Beak
relatively long and dagger-
like. Moves actively on tree
trunks and branches, both
head-up and head-down,
unlike woodpeckers. Call a
distinctive, far-carrying,
ringing 'chwit'; song a
repetitive 'toowee toowee'.
Inhabits mature deciduous
woodland and parkland.
Widespread, locally common.

Red-backed Shrike *Lanius collurio* 18cm Small, colourful shrike. Adult male has a chestnut-brown back; crown and nape dove-grey; rump grey and tail black with white edges. Black patch through eye. Throat white, rest of underparts white, tinged pinkish-buff. Female dull brown above with dark brown eyepatch, whitish below with fine bars. Beak dark, large and conspicuously hooked. Immature resembles female, but with heavy scaly markings. Call a harsh 'chack'; song a melodious warble. Inhabits dryish open country with bushes or scrub, heathland. Widespread.

Jay *Garrulus glandarius* 35cm Medium-sized, brightly-coloured crow. Adult and immature have rich pinkish-buff upperparts with chestnut shading; rump white, tail black. Wings blackish, with bold white wingbar and bright blue patch conspicuous at 'wrist'. Underparts pale pinkish-buff. Crown pinkish with black flecks, raised as short crest if excited. Black moustachial stripes. Eye pale pink. Beak dark grey, stout. Flight floppy on erratically beating, rounded, fingered wings. Noisy: call a harsh 'skaark'; song a subdued mixture of cackling notes, rarely heard. Inhabits woods, farmland and parkland with plentiful trees. Widespread, often quite common.

Crows

Rook *Corvus frugilegus* 45cm
Medium-large crow. Adult male and female have whole plumage glossy black with iridescent sheen. Upper leg (thigh) feathers loose and rough, giving 'baggy-trousered' appearance (*see* Carrion Crow). Beak pale, running to whitish cheek-patches; long, dagger-shaped. Immature has duller sooty-black plumage; beak blackish; lacks cheek-patches. Colonial when breeding and gregarious feeding, often with Jackdaws. Noisy: call a raucous 'carr'. Inhabits arable farmland with adjacent woodland or plenty of tall trees. Widespread, often common.

Jackdaw *Corvus monedula* 33cm
One of the smaller crows. Adult and immature have most of head and body dull sooty black; crown, nape and upper breast have variable amount of grey. Eye startlingly white. Beak relatively short but stout. Gregarious: often in large flocks with Rooks. Flight usually direct, with quicker wingbeats than other crows, and lacking fingered wingtips. Vocal: call a metallic 'jack'. Inhabits open woodland, parkland, farmland and urban areas, often nesting colonially in old trees or ruined buildings. Widespread, often common.

Magpie *Pica pica* 45cm Long-tailed, pied crow. Adult and immature have black back and upper breast; belly white; wings black and white; tail black with purple and green iridescence, long and tapered. Head and nape glossy black. Immature when freshly fledged is duller and with rather shorter tail. Flight direct but on fluttering, rounded wings. Call a harsh chatter; song a surprisingly musical, quiet collection of piping notes, not often heard. Inhabits woodland, parkland, farmland, heath and scrub, mature gardens, even city-centre parks. Widespread, locally numerous.

Carrion Crow *Corvus corone* 45cm One of the larger crows. Adult and immature wholly black. Upper leg (thigh) feathers neatly close-fitting (*see* Rook). Beak black; stout with convex upper mandible; black feathers at base (*see* Rook). Only occasionally gregarious. Voice a deep, harsh 'caw' or 'corr'. Inhabits open countryside of all types with suitable tall trees for nesting, also urban areas, even city centres. Widespread but rarely very numerous.

Starling *Sturnus vulgaris* 22cm Small. Summer adult plumage blackish, glossily iridescent at close range; back has bright buffish flecks. Beak yellow with blue base in male, pink in female. Legs pinkish-brown. Winter adult lacks much of the iridescence; heavily spotted with white. Immature uniformly drab brown. Gregarious, often in huge flocks. Flight swift and direct, characteristic triangular wing silhouette. Noisy: calls include harsh shrieks and scolding chattering; song extended and varied, including much expert mimicry of other birds, often accompanied by wing-flapping display on perch. Habitat widely varied. Mostly abundant. Common.

Greenfinch *Carduelis chloris* 15cm Small finch with robust beak. Summer adult male olive-green above, grey on nape and cheeks. Wings brown with bold yellow patches conspicuous in flight; tail brown with yellow patch on either side of base. Underparts largely rich yellow. Beak pale, comparatively large, triangular. Winter male and female brownish-olive, less dramatic yellow patches in wings and tail. Immature similar, but with narrow brown streaks on back and flanks. Call a drawling 'dwee-ee'; song an extended purring trill, often given in display flight. Inhabits woodland, farmland, parks and gardens. Widespread, often numerous.

Chaffinch *Fringilla coelebs* 15cm
Small finch. Adult male
rufous-brown on back; wings
dark brown, with two white
wingbars; tail blackish
showing white outer feathers.
Underparts rich pink, shading
to white on lower belly. Head
and nape grey, forehead black.
Winter plumage subdued.
Beak grey, comparatively
long. Female and immature
brown above, pale fawn
below; wings brownish
showing wingbars; tail dark
brown, white-edged. Often
gregarious in winter. Flight
deeply undulating, wingbars
conspicuous. Call a ringing
'pink'; song a descending
cascade ending in flourish.
Inhabits woodland, farmland,
parks and gardens.
Widespread, common.

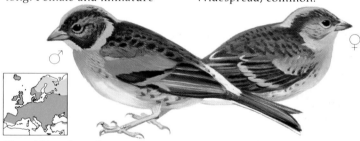

Brambling *Fringilla
montifringilla* 15cm Small,
colourful finch. Summer adult
male largely glossy black on
head and back; wings dark
brown, with orange forewing
and white wingbar; tail
blackish. Throat and breast
bright orange, shading to
white on belly. Winter male
plumage obscured by buff
scaly markings. Female and
immature mottled brown and
blackish above, pale orange-
brown below. Often
gregarious in winter. In flight,
wingbar and white rump-
patch conspicuous. Call a
flourishing 'tchway', often
given in flight; song a series of
'twee' notes. Inhabits
woodland, farmland and parks
in winter. Widespread;
variable numbers.

Finches

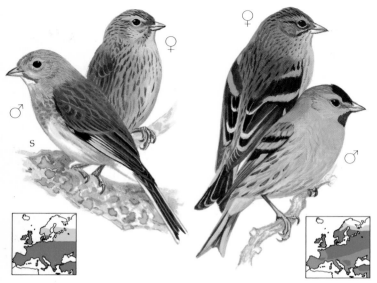

Linnet *Carduelis cannabina* 13cm
Small brown finch. Summer adult male has rich chestnut back; wings brown, with poorly defined white patch; rump whitish; tail black with white edge. Head and underparts pale fawn, with variable areas of glossy pink on crown and breast. Winter male, female and immature dull brown, paler below than on back, with brown streaks and lacking pink patches. Beak blackish, stubby. Gregarious. Flight deeply undulating. Call a penetrating 'tsweet'; song a musical and varied twittering often given from prominent perch. Inhabits heath, scrub and farmland, occasionally parks and gardens. Widespread, locally common.

Siskin *Carduelis spinus* 12cm
Tiny dark finch. Adult male greenish on upperparts, often heavily streaked with black. Wings dark brown; double yellowish wingbars. Crown and small bib black, underparts yellowish shading to white on belly, flanks streaked with brown. Female and immature duller and browner; brown streaking above and below. Beak dark, relatively long, pointed at tip. In flight, yellow rump and yellow patches beside base of dark, deeply forked tail conspicuous. Call, often given in flight, a wheezy 'chwee-oo'; song a prolonged twittering. Inhabits woodland, parks, occasionally gardens. Widespread, sometimes common.

Goldfinch *Carduelis carduelis* 13cm Small colourful finch. Adult male and female unmistakable, with harlequin plumage. Crown and nape black, face red and white. Wings black; broad gold wingbars are distinctive in flight, as is white rump contrasting with black tail. Beak whitish with dark tip, relatively long and pointed for a finch. Immature is paler and buffer, with plain buff head. Call a distinctive 'dee-dee-lit'; song a prolonged, liquid warbling twitter. Inhabits open woodland, heath, scrub, farmland, parks and gardens. Widespread, locally common.

Redpoll *Carduelis flammea* 12cm Small dark finch. Adult male and female have brown upperparts with blackish streaking; underparts buffish, paling to white on belly. Small black bib. Forehead and crown have characteristic small red patch. Summer male may have pinkish flush on breast. Immature duller, lacking bib and red 'poll'. Several geographical races occur: northern birds tend to be paler and slightly larger than southern ones. Call 'chee-chee-chit'; song a distinctive, high-pitched, purring trill, often delivered in circling song-flight high above woodland. Inhabits mixed woodland (favouring birch), farmland and well-treed scrub. Fairly common.

Bullfinch *Pyrrhula pyrrhula*
15cm Small heavy-headed
finch. Adult male has bold
black cap, dove-grey mantle
and back, striking white rump
contrasting with black tail.
Wings black; bold white
wingbar. Underparts rich pink
to crimson, shading to white
on belly. Beak black, rounded.
Female has black cap, grey-
brown mantle and back; wing
and rump patterns as male.
Underparts soft fawn.
Immature similar to female,
lacking black cap. Flight
hesitant, deeply undulating.
Call a distinctive whistle
'peeu'; song a rarely-heard,
quiet creaking warble.
Inhabits woodland, scrub,
parks, farmland and gardens.
Widespread, but rarely
numerous.

Yellowhammer *Emberiza
citrinella* 18cm Small bunting.
Summer male has back, rump
and wings rich chestnut,
streaked with black and
brown. Tail dark with whitish
outer feathers; relatively long.
Head and neck bright yellow;
variable black markings on
head. Breast and belly canary
yellow, tinged chestnut on
breast and flanks. Winter male
much browner. Female and
immature streaked brown
above chestnut rump. Head
yellowish, with dark streaking;
underparts pale yellow, white
on belly, streaked brown on
flanks and breast. Call a sharp
'twick'; song a series of 'zit'
notes, ending in wheezy
'zeee'. Inhabits heath, scrub
and farmland. Widespread,
often common.

Reed Bunting *Emberiza schoeniclus* 15cm Small bunting. Summer male has rich brown back with darker streaks; grey-brown rump; blackish tail with white outer feathers. Crown and face black; white collar running into white moustachial streaks and whitish underparts; throat and upper breast black. Winter plumage obscured by buff feather fringes. Female and immature brown above, buff below; dark streaks on back and flanks. Crown rich brown, separated from dark cheek-patch by buffish eyestripe; adjacent whitish and black moustachial streaks. Call 'tsee-you'; song short harsh, discordant. Inhabits marshes, scrub and farmland. Widespread, often common.

Corn Bunting *Miliaria calandra* 18cm One of the larger, and certainly most nondescript, European buntings. Adult and immature relatively plump; dark sandy-brown above, paler sandy-brown below, paling to white on the belly, with copious brown streaks. Tail dark brown, lacking white outer feathers. Call a short 'tsrip' or disyllabic 'tsip-ip'; song characteristic, an unmistakable harsh, metallic jangling, delivered from prominent song-post. Inhabits open, dry farmland, heath and scrub. Widespread but with large local variations in numbers.

Sparrows

House Sparrow *Passer domesticus*
15cm Small, with triangular
beak. Adult male has rich
brown back with darker
brown streaks. Wings brown
with double white wingbar.
Rump dark grey-buff; tail
blackish. Crown grey and
nape rich dark chestnut;
cheeks whitish; throat and
upper breast black, rest of
underparts whitish. Female
and immature sandy-brown
above, with darker brown
markings and clear buff
eyestripe. Underparts pale
grey-buff. Beak relatively
long, blackish in male,
brownish in female.
Gregarious. Call a clear
'chirrup'; song a monotonous
chirruping. Frequents human
habitats. Widespread, often
numerous.

Tree Sparrow *Passer montanus*
13cm Small, with triangular
beak. Adult male and female
similar. Upperparts rich
brown mottled with black
streaks. Crown and nape pale
chestnut; characteristic white
cheeks with central black spot.
Small black bib, with rest of
underparts off-white. Beak
black and stubby. Immature
drabber, less clearly marked.
Gregarious, but not to same
extent as House. Calls include
short metallic 'chip' and 'chop',
and a repeated 'chit-tchup'.
Distinctive liquid flight-call,
'tek, tek', is difficult to
describe but diagnostic once
learnt. Frequents woodland,
well-treed farmland and
scrub, usually distant from
habitation. Widespread.

Further Reading

There is an enormous number of bird books available, of which the following is a useful selection.

Campbell, B. and Lack, E. (Eds), *A Dictionary of Birds*. T.& A.D. Poyser, Calton, 1985.

Cramp, S. and Simmons, K.E.L. (Eds), *Handbook of the Birds of Europe, the Middle East and Africa* (vols. I-V published to date). Oxford University Press, Oxford, 1977.

Fisher, J. and Flegg, J., *Watching Birds*. Penguin Books, Harmondsworth, 1978.

Flegg, J., *In Search of Birds; Their Haunts and Habitats*. Blandford Press, Poole, 1983.

Flegg, J., *Birdlife*. Pelham Books, London, 1986.

Harrison, P., *Seabirds – An Identification Guide*. Croom Helm, London, 1985.

Hayman, P., Marchant, J. and Prater, T., *Shorebirds – An Identification Guide*. Croom Helm, London, 1986.

Jellis, R., *Bird Sounds and Their Meaning*. BBC Publications, London, 1977.

Madge, S., *Wildfowl: An Identification Guide to the Ducks, Geese and Swans of the World*. Christopher Helm, London, 1988.

Mead, C., *Bird Migration*. Country Life Books, London, 1983.

Ogilvie, M., *The Wildfowl of Britain and Europe*. Oxford University Press, Oxford, 1982.

Useful Addresses

British Ornithologists' Union (BOU)
c/o Zoological Society of London, Regent's Park, London
NW1 4RY.

British Trust for Ornithology (BTO)
Beech Grove, Station Road, Tring, Herts HP23 5NR.

British Waterfowl Association
6 Caldicott Close, Over, Windsford, Cheshire CW7 1LW.

Hawk Trust
c/o Birds of Prey Section, Zoological Society of London,
Regent's Park, London NW1 4RY.

National Trust
36 Queen Anne's Gate, London SW1H 9AS.

National Trust for Scotland
5 Charlotte Square, Edinburgh EH2 4DU.

Royal Society for the Protection of Birds (RSPB)
The Lodge, Sandy, Beds SG19 2DL.

Scottish Ornithologists' Club
21 Regent Terrace, Edinburgh EH7 5BT.

Wildfowl and Wetland Trust
Gatehouse, Slimbridge, Glos GL2 7BT.

In Britain, most counties have a County Naturalists' Trust,
which is responsible for the management of various
reserves (though not all of them are for birds), and an
ornithological society. Addresses of such organisations can
be obtained from local libraries.

Index

Index